LEGENDARY SANTA'S

Stories from the Chair

By Leeanne Meadows Ladin

First Printing

Copyright © 2011 by The Children's Museum of Richmond

All rights reserved. No part of this book may be reproduced or transmitted in any form or by any means, electronically or mechanical, including photocopying, recording, or by any information storage and retrieval system, without the written permission of the Publisher.

Author:

Leeanne Meadows Ladin

Publisher/photographer:

Wayne Dementi

Dementi Milestone Publishing, Inc.

Manakin-Sabot, VA 23103

www.dementimilestonepublishing.com

Cataloging-in-publication data for this book is available from The Library of Congress.

ISBN: 978-0-9827019-9-7

Graphic design/photography by:

Jayne E. Hushen

Hushen Design & Photography

Printed in China

Attempts have been made to identify the owners of any copyrighted materials appearing in this book. The Publisher extends his apology for any errors or omissions and encourages copyright owners inadvertently missed to contact him.

Little Betty Jane Rowe gazes at Legendary Santa for the first time.
Photo courtesy of Dan Rowe.

Table of Contents

Acknowledgements
vi

Dedication
vii

Preface
viii

Foreword
x

Chapter 1   "You're Really Real!"
1

Chapter 2   Santa Claus Is Coming to Town
21

Chapter 3   Making a List and Checking It Twice
35

Chapter 4   Favorite Memories of the Snow Queens
47

Chapter 5   Tea with Santa…Coming Full Circle
59

Chapter 6   Santa's Favorite Stories from the Chair
77

Chapter 7   Yes, Virginia, There is a Santa Claus
109

Acknowledgements

Though most of Santa's helpers live at the North Pole, we found many of them right here in Richmond, ready and willing to assist us with producing this book!

You contributed in a variety of ways: through personal interviews, phone calls, emails, research assistance and through the Children's Museum's website and Facebook page. You shared your precious memories, your photos and clippings and most of all, your sense of what makes Legendary Santa so special. Many of you are pictured or mentioned in the book. Please know you have our sincere gratitude.

We do want to name some very special contributors who truly made this book possible: Dan Rowe, Jeff Beatman, Charlie Nuckols, Allan Rothert, Robin Hood, Carolyn Hood Drudge and the the beautiful Snow Queens. We also thank John Cario of the Hilton Garden Inn, Debo Dabney, Desiree Roots, Milton Burke, the Cobb family, Hermie and Angie Sadler, and especially the Perrin family for all they shared with us. We appreciate the endorsements by Alice Goodwin, Cindy Harrison and Paul Levengood. Santa has something extra for the stocking of book designer Jayne Hushen, who once again worked her inimitable magic and vibrantly brought this story to life on the page. We especially thank Herb Wimble IV for his wonderful illustrations. And again, we are indebted to the resources of the Times Dispatch, the Valentine Richmond History Center and Frank Dementi's Colonial Studio.

We especially want to thank the Children's Museum of Richmond for the privilege of producing this milestone book for Legendary's Santa 75th Anniversary. It was a joy to work with Karen Coltrane, Lisa Wingfield Hailey, Michelle Rosman and Suzie Zeh. This book was Lisa Hailey's baby. Like Rudolph guiding Santa's sleigh, Lisa was a shining beacon guiding this from start to finish with her strong, heartfelt vision of capturing not only the historic legacy of Legendary Santa, but the emotional impact as well. She set a new measure of success for us. If a chapter made her cry, we'd done our job!

Finally, we are forever grateful to Legendary Santa. He gave us the greatest gift of all… himself. He took us down an enchanted memory lane filled with snowflakes, elves, snow queens and sleigh bells, showing us along the way that the true spirit of Christmas shines all year with every unselfish act of love, kindness and compassion.

We were deeply honored to be his faithful scribe and can only hope that this book pays sufficient tribute to the joyous and generous spirit of Richmond's own Legendary Santa.

Leeanne Meadows Ladin

Dedication

*"Yes, Virginia, there is a Santa Claus.
He exists as certainly as love and generosity and devotion exist…"*

— from the New York Sun 1897.

This book is dedicated to everyone who keeps Santa in their hearts all year long. As Legendary Santa has taught us, when you give a gift, material or intangible, freely and with love, then you are a Santa too!

PREFACE

Dear Santa – How'd you know my name?

The magic seems to begin with the smile on a child's face when Santa calls out his name as the child makes his way toward him. Since this book presents Stories From the Chair, I wanted to ask Santa just how he knows everyone's name. So, I called him to see what he would say… I said "Santa ~ how do you know all the children's names?" His answer:

"Why….. because I'm Santa," he said. "I know all my children's names. I need to know because I must know who's been naughty and nice." Then he thought for a second, and added… "You know, now that I think about it, I don't think I have ever run across a child who had been naughty all year."

Much has been written about Legendary Santa. Most all of these accounts have shared Santa stories from the viewpoint of the child, or from an observer of Santa and his history. Our task, with Stories From the Chair, is to share with you what Santa has to say about the past 75 years. His words become even more meaningful when we note that along the way, he was dubbed Legendary. Our conversations with Santa reveal that he accepts this designation with a keen sense of responsibility. To say that he works hard to maintain the "magic" would be a large understatement.

When I was a youngster, I had the opportunity of observing our Legendary Santa from a privileged position. My father, Frank Dementi, was asked to photograph Santa every year. So, I would accompany him on his trips to Miller & Rhoads….to photograph the magical Christmas windows, the Santa Teas and Santa's travels. The magic was as real behind the scenes as it was when I sat on his lap.

We are indeed privileged to have The Legendary Santa right here. On behalf of all of us, I am honored to extend our appreciation to the Children's Museum of Richmond for seeing that current and future generations enjoy the Magic of Legendary Santa. We sincerely hope you will find that Santa's Stories From the Chair affirms every childhood belief you hold about his contribution to the joy of Christmas.

Wayne Dementi, Publisher

Little Jack Nelson runs across the stage into Santa's arms.

FOREWORD

Merry Christmas and hello to all my babies!

It's hard to believe that it's been 75 years since I first visited the Miller & Rhoads department store in downtown Richmond, Virginia. I've seen "my babies" grow up, and now you're bringing your babies and even grandbabies to see me, even from out-of-town and out-of-state. Sometimes we have four generations of a family in one picture! As I like to say, "Santa is for every child and child at heart!"

We've created many special memories together over the years. So, what better way to celebrate my 75th anniversary in Richmond than with your favorite stories about Legendary Santa and my favorite stories about you! That's why I was so pleased to work with the Children's Museum of Richmond (my permanent home when I'm not at the North Pole) on this compilation of "Stories from the Chair."

I think you'll see that this book is not only about memories. It's very much about gifts. Not just the toys I bring or the treats for your children's stockings. It's about the gifts of family togetherness, of tradition, of love and generosity and sharing. Gifts which we should exchange all year long, not just during the holidays.

Now, don't forget, I'll be coming down the chimney soon. So be as good as you can and remember, Old Santa loves you!

Legendary Santa

LEGENDARY SANTA'S STORIES FROM THE CHAIR

"You're Really Real!"

November 26, 2010 at The Children's Museum of Richmond…

It's the day after Thanksgiving. Hundreds of Richmonders and even out-of-towners have gotten up at the crack of dawn, bundled up and bolted out the door. They are about to take part in an annual ritual that dates back for decades. For many, this day heralds the start of the holiday season and they wouldn't dream of missing it. The custom, to which they devote great planning and preparation, is so deeply embedded in their lives that it is passed on from one generation to the next.

No, they are not flocking to the shopping malls for the much-hyped holiday sales. They have come to one location to see one man, the one timeless figure who embodies the spirit of Christmas, the one whose authenticity is unquestioned. They have come to see Richmond's Legendary Santa.

The museum lobby is thronged with children and parents waiting in a long line that stretches to the door. Christmas colors abound with little girls dressed in red and burgundy party frocks, and boys smartly attired in green or red vests. The feeling of good cheer is evident in the crowd. They know their patience will soon be rewarded, for they are about to cross the threshold into a magical realm that evokes childlike wonder at any age and where memories crystallize like snowflakes that never melt.

The doors to Santa Land fling open and the room quickly fills. The eager youngsters sit on the edge of their seats by their parents, trying mightily to stay on their very best behavior. Some kids have wiggled into positions at the foot of the stage, their expectant faces turned up to where a large, ornate golden throne sits empty, awaiting its celebrated occupant. Giant teddy bears benevolently stand guard throughout the room. The Christmas tree lights are twinkling and the Snow Queen's chair glitters like frost. The buzz of excitement hangs in the air.

Suddenly the Elf appears, an impish figure in red and green with comical curled up shoes and a jingle bell hat. "Boys and girls, are you excited to see Santa?" she asks with a knowing grin.

LEGENDARY SANTA'S STORIES FROM THE CHAIR

The room erupts in a resounding "YES!" – then immediately falls silent as sleigh bells jingle in the distance. Not a person is stirring as the sound grows closer and closer. Santa's sleigh must have landed on the roof! All eyes are fixed on the fireplace and chimney. The hush is broken with a collective gasp as a pair of large black boots come into view, dangling in the air. They thump to the ground and the crowd sees red velvet pants, then the thick white fur trim of a coat.

At last, Legendary Santa appears in full view before the cheering crowd. His flowing beard is snowy white against his red velvet coat. His ruddy-cheeked face beams at the crowd and his eyes are twinkling merrily.

"Hello, my babies! Merry Christmas! I'm so glad to see you!" he exclaims with open arms.

And Richmonders who have embraced Legendary Santa for over seven decades are equally glad to see him.

Thus another holiday season begins with a beloved icon. Though the location of Santa Land has changed more than once since Legendary Santa first visited Miller & Rhoads in 1936, one thing has remained constant…the heartfelt and enduring belief that he is the real Santa Claus.

Just as he calls each of his reindeer by name, he will soon be greeting each child by name as they walk up to his chair to whisper their Christmas wishes. This small gesture has made a lasting impact for generations. It is why more than one incredulous child has exclaimed after Santa gently hoisted her onto his knee, "You're really real!"

Legendary Santa knows he has legions of true believers. He knows that many drive hundreds of miles to see him. He knows that many who sat on his knee as children now bring their children and grandchildren to see him.

"I want to share some of YOUR stories in appreciation for making me a part of your lives," Santa said. "And it seems most fitting that the first story should come from the family who has been first in line for the last twenty years!"

LEGENDARY SANTA'S STORIES FROM THE CHAIR

Candice Cobb didn't get to see Legendary Santa on her first visit at fifteen months of age in 1983. Her parents, Bentley and Pam, took her on the day after Thanksgiving and when they found out it would be a six hour wait, they went back home. In 1986, with her new baby brother (also named Bentley) in tow, they hit on the right formula to guarantee they would be first in line.

"We will NEVER tell the real time we got there," Candice said, "but we stood out in the cold until the security guard got there and let us in."

From that year on, the Cobb family has held fast to their ritual. Traveling from their Chester home, they claim their spot, braving the cold, fortified with warm doughnuts from the nearby Krispy Kreme. They have been joined by another family, the Harrisons, who stake out the second-in-line territory. The payoff comes in one simple phrase: "Now Candice and Bentley, come over and sit in old Santa's lap."

Candice Cobb and her family have been first in line to see Santa for many years. Photo courtesy of Cobb family.

Bentley Cobb (senior) disclosed a few of the escapades the family has experienced in their quest to be first in line.

"One year at Sixth Street Marketplace, we got there before the security guard and I thought I'd just walk around and jiggle the doors to see if one might be open. One was!" he laughed. "It was right by the shoeshine station, so I went on in. I sat by the entrance to Santa Land and waited. When the security guard got there, he read me the riot act!" But once again the family was first in line.

The next year (around 1995) Mr. Cobb took an even bigger risk. "I jiggled the doors again and the door of the bank by the building was open. So I walked through the bank, with all its security cameras, and over to Sixth Street Marketplace." The security guard saw him but had no questions, so perhaps the Cobbs' reputation had preceded them.

That was certainly the case at the Richmond Convention Center, when it became the home of Legendary Santa.

"The security people already knew about us," Bentley said. "They let us in before the doors were supposed to open."

3

LEGENDARY SANTA'S STORIES FROM THE CHAIR

Even though Candice Cobb and her brother Bentley have grown up, they still want to see Santa. Photo courtesy of Cobb family

The Cobbs have had few to challenge their first-in-line tradition. However, Bentley noted that one year a man tried to run around the door to beat the Cobbs when Santa was at Thalhimers. "Everyone yelled at the guy," Bentley said. "We still ended up first!"

Though his children are grown up now, Bentley says "They are still into Legendary Santa. Bentley is the first to ask if we're going to see Santa. Candice, who is a school teacher, tells her students that she is going to see the Real Santa."

Bentley adds that after the visit, "My family comes home and we get out all of the old videos and DVDs from the years past. As a family, we sit down and watch each one just to see what we asked for and to keep the tradition going."

Troy Harrison of the second-in-line family noted that "There have been others who have tried to beat us, but with no success. They would ask what time we got here but we'd always deceive them!"

He said that when his mother died of cancer in 1997, he and his brother pledged to keep the tradition going. They join in on the Krispy Kreme stop and meet the Cobbs at McLean's restaurant after seeing Santa. The ritual has led to a friendship with the Cobbs, extending to going to high school football games and other activities. Their friendship became an unexpected gift stemming from a shared holiday ritual.

This little girl is pointing the way to Santa Land at Miller & Rhoads. Photo courtesy of Beth Stell.

"For many families, coming to see me is not as simple as driving across town. It's more like a pilgrimage," said Legendary Santa.

That was certainly true for Paige Morgan of Emporia who used to dress her girls in the car on the way to Richmond on the day after Thanksgiving.

5

"We would leave Emporia at 5:45 am to be sure to get in line and see Santa come down the chimney at 9:00. The girls would get in the car in their pajamas and I'd feed them breakfast. Then I would dress them in their Christmas dresses with their little pearl necklaces and bracelets," Paige said.

She remembers seeing the same people in line year after year, including one man who told her, "You do not know how much I have enjoyed watching your children grow up."

Even when the location of Santa's Richmond home kept changing, the Morgans followed him. As the girls began to wonder about his "realness," his cheery greeting of "Well, Heather and Lindsey, you all did make it from Emporia!" dispelled all doubts. The youngest girl was so enamored of Santa that when she turned two, she declared that she wanted not a regular birthday cake, but a Reindeer Cake, like the ones served at the Santa Teas.

Leigh Brooks Davis Rooke and her family used to drive eight hours from Asheville, N.C. to stay with family in Richmond and go see Legendary Santa. She had a very special connection to the jolly old elf. Her great grandfather was Absalom B. Laughon, who was president of Miller & Rhoads from 1942 – 1944.

Leigh remembers getting a store discount and buying her Christmas outfit to see Legendary Santa. "For my family," she said, "it was not a question of IF we'll go, it was WHEN we'd go to see Legendary Santa!"

Jane Plum (the wife of Virginia Delegate Ken Plum) is used to driving a long distance to see Legendary Santa. Her family lived in Essex County and made the annual trip to Richmond to see Legendary Santa, sparking memories that have lasted a lifetime.

"He knew my name," she said. "I believed for longer than anyone I know, and I suppose that was the reason; the real Santa knew my name."

When she had her own children, she began making the trek from Springfield in Northern Virginia in 1977.

Jane Durham Plum and brother Chuck. Photo courtesy of Jane Plum.

LEGENDARY SANTA'S STORIES FROM THE CHAIR

The trip became an even bigger family affair that has at times included her brother Chuck's children, cousins from Nashville, Tennessee and a cousin from Burke in Northern Virginia.

The entourage continues to expand with the grandchildren from Fredericksburg and Essex now coming with their "Nana Jane" and her 92-year-old mother Ella Durham to Richmond. Four generations coming to see Legendary Santa at the Children's Museum. "We would not think of being anywhere else!" said Jane.

Patti Leonard (now Lacy) and her sister Cathy visited Legendary Santa at Miller & Rhoads as little girls. Decades later, Patti would continue the tradition and bring her four boys, even letting them miss a day of school! She said:

"Our boys loved Christmas and they still do. We had many Christmas traditions and missing a day from school to see Santa was one of them. Some of them wrote letters to Santa and gave them to him that day or mailed it to the North Pole earlier in December. They all decorated their room with lights and decorations. We always went to see Bruce the Spruce and the boys did some shopping at the Fawn Shop. We had lunch in the Tea Room and watched Santa and his entourage eating lunch. They were always anxious to get some Reindeer Cake from Santa also."

"Some of my visitors tell me they even play hooky from school to come see me," Santa laughed. "I guess it's OK as long as the parents and teachers don't mind!"

In 1988, Patti's son Ross at 12 months was not so complacent! Also pictured (in stairstep order) are Matthew, Graham and Andrew Lacy.

Patti Leonard Lacy, 10 months old with her sister Cathy, was pretty calm at seeing Santa for the first time in 1953.

LEGENDARY SANTA'S STORIES FROM THE CHAIR

Melissa Face sometimes got to play hooky, with the approval of her mother and her teachers. It was only once a year, when she and her family would make their annual trip from Wakefield to Miller & Rhoads. "The teachers knew we were going to see the real Santa!" Melissa explained.

Other times, Melissa and her sister got up before the sun on a Saturday and put on their shiny patent leather shoes and Christmas dresses (with their mom's help.) After their aunts and cousins congregated at the house, they all embarked on the hour-long drive to Richmond. In the car, the cousins carefully rehearsed their Christmas lists for their big moment with Legendary Santa.

"Over the course of several years, we asked him for bicycles, doll babies that talked and walked and various other toys," Melissa recalled. She added that Santa would typically say, "We'll see what old Santa can do." Then, clutching their candy canes and coloring books, she and her cousins would be on their way.

" I often think about those enchanting trips to Santa Land and how wonderful it was that Mom always arranged for us to have a piece of the magic," she said.

"Sometimes the children have a lot of questions about me," Santa said. "Those questions can be hard to answer. I try to offer a little help when I can!"

At one point in her childhood, Mythica von Griffyn had her doubts about Legendary Santa. She and her brother were always amazed that Santa knew their names and wanted to trip him up somehow. But in 1976, Mythica got all the proof she needed that this was the real Santa.

"It was my birthday," she said. "We went to have Reindeer Cake in Miller & Rhoads. We were way in the back, and I asked to go see the organ player. Santa was sitting up at the table, with the Snow Queen and Elves. While I was just randomly there, Santa called me over from the organ player... and he wished me a happy birthday!!! It was a chance encounter! How did he know!?!? I tell everyone he's the real Santa! Because of him, I will ALWAYS believe!"

Mythica and her brother Noel, 1974. Photo courtesy of Mythica von Griffyn.

Cayley Shriner and Jack Nelson share their Christmas lists with Santa.

Owen Gorey was not too happy to see Santa. Photo courtesy of Mrs. Gorey

Little Owen Gorey had lots of questions about Legendary Santa. When he was four, he began to pepper his mother with questions:

"How does Santa do it? Does he stop time? Does he eat cookies on every stop or does he get them to go? Do you think Santa repairs roofs during the summer? If I eat only magic reindeer oatmeal from now on will I be able to fly? Does Santa really know the name of every kid in the world?"

As Owen climbed into Santa's lap that year, Legendary Santa said, "Well hello Owen, I am so glad that you've come to visit me again this year."

On the drive home, a quiet Owen said, "Mom, Santa does know the name of every kid in the world. Santa knows my name."

Kristin Alexander, who had been going to see Santa since she was nine months old, admitted, "Somewhere along the line, I stopped believing in Santa Claus."

Kristin Alexander's belief in Santa was renewed after the birth of her daughter. Photo courtesy of Kristin Alexander.

It was a gradual process, she noted. But the clincher came in the fifth grade. She had been boasting about getting out of school early to go see Santa Claus when a "beady-eyed, freckle-faced kid" said to her, "You know Santa's not real, right?" The seed of doubt blossomed into full-blown skepticism.

Time went by. Miller & Rhoads closed and Kristin moved away and got married. She noted, "As the years passed, and I was caught up in holiday stress and demands, I remembered less and less about why I once loved Christmas so much."

Then, in December 2010, Kristin and her family arrived in Richmond for the holidays. She went to see Legendary Santa for the first time since 1988, this time with her one-year-old daughter.

LEGENDARY SANTA'S STORIES FROM THE CHAIR

It marked the third generation of family visits to see the "real" Santa Claus in downtown Richmond.

"It's a tradition I look forward to continuing with my daughter, and one that I hope she'll love as much as I did growing up," Kristin said.

"And just like that, I believe in Santa again!"

Legendary Santa left no doubt in the minds of Linda B. Harris' girls. In fact he left quite an "impression." Linda's story starts with a happy coincidence.

"Little did I realize that when I married my husband and we combined our photos of Santa, that he and I had been waiting in the same line to see "The Santa" when we were in first grade together," she said.

They later married, had two daughters and of course, took them to see Legendary Santa. At one point, the older daughter started asking questions about Santa, but her parents did not want her to spoil it for her younger sister. That year, Santa told the girls, with a wink to Linda and her husband, that when they awoke on Christmas morning to check their foreheads to see if there was a "soot fingerprint." If so, they would know that he had been to see them.

On Christmas Day, the girls jumped out of bed and there on their foreheads was "his fingerprint." And so the magic continued.

Many other families recounted their "sooty" fingerprint stories as well, including the Ellett family pictured above.

The Ellett children often found a "sooty fingerprint" on their foreheads on Christmas morning, proof positive that Legendary Santa had been to see them. Photo courtesy of the Ellett family.

Susan Brooks Diggles of Glen Allen became a true believer when she was about three years old. She explained that she and her sister, ages three and five respectively, were making their yearly visit to see Santa at Miller & Rhoads. It started off as usual, seeing the Snow Queen, telling Santa what they wanted for Christmas.

But as they were leaving, Santa said, "Now, Susan, I don't want to see you sucking your thumb when I come to your house on Christmas Eve." Susan said her parents were floored. "I only sucked my thumb when I went to bed, never in public. How did he know I sucked my thumb?" she marveled. Evidently, there must be something to those song lyrics, "he sees you when you're sleeping..."

This little tyke seems to be trying to find out if Santa's beard is real. Photo courtesy of Valentine Richmond History Center. Circa 1958.

LEGENDARY SANTA'S STORIES FROM THE CHAIR

Despite her crying in this photo, Julie Addington had fond memories of going to see Legendary Santa when she was a child. She couldn't wait to take her son to see the real Santa. "You can see that twinkle in his eyes. His kindness, gentleness and love for the children embody what makes the Christmas season special," she said. Julie Addington in 1967 (pictured left) and son Joshua in 2004 (pictured right). Photos courtesy of Julie Addington.

Michele Rodriguez said she "cried like a baby" when she took her son to see Santa for the first time. "My mother and father were with me and my son, and they couldn't decide whose reaction was more priceless, mine or his!"

She explained that she was adopted at age five after having lived in a Mennonite foster home which was very strict. Her adoptive mother, who happily embraced Christmas, made seeing Legendary Santa an annual tradition. "I think the reason I cried is because I have such overwhelming emotions when it comes to the happiness I had as a child because of the wonderful parents I got to choose and who chose me."

"I am very touched by how the photos and videos from a visit with me can become very important keepsakes," said Santa.

For Beth Stell, the photos and videos made of her family with Santa hold special meaning. She and her sister would go downtown to Miller & Rhoads to see Santa after school. She recalls, "After my sister and I would see Santa,

Beth Stell and her sister, 1989. Photo courtesy of Beth Stell.

my Mom would always sit in Santa's lap and talk to him and give him a hug. My grandmother had taken her to see Santa at Miller & Rhoads when she was a child. We still have photos and movies of Mom sitting in Santa's lap and telling him what she wanted for Christmas.

Mom died when I was twelve years old, so having these photos and movies of her with Legendary Santa mean so much to us."

"Once in awhile, children need a reminder that Santa knows when they've been naughty or nice," Santa said.

This was borne out when the Miller family took their boys to see Legendary Santa. It was Christmas 1970 and the boys, Bart, age nine, and Bruce, age seven, had been rough-housing. Their scuffle, which left Bart with a scratch under his eye, actually began over an argument as to whether Santa was real.

When they approached Santa, he said, "Bart and Bruce, have you have been fighting again? I thought you were going to be good this year!"

From that moment (until Christmas day, at least) their mother says they were as good as gold, and so was their belief in Legendary Santa.

Bart (left) and Bruce Miller with Santa. You can see the scratch under Bart's eye. Photo courtesy of the Miller family.

Little Blakely Koob from Fredericksburg may have struggled to answer Santa truthfully when he asked if she'd been a good girl.

"Last year I took my children to visit Legendary Santa for the first time," Blakely's mother said. My son, Billy, was eight; my daughter, Blakely, was four. I explained to them how this was the same Santa I used to visit when I was little, and that I thought it would be neat for us to visit. I so wish that I had been able to bring them since Billy was a baby, but my husband was in the military, and this was the first opportunity I had to visit.

When we first pulled into the parking lot, I did not see the line, so was I hoping it would be a short wait. Then we got inside the shelter! After a couple of hours, we made it in for our visit. I must admit that seeing Santa again took my breath away. I still remember looking at the Nutcracker displays on my visits to Santa when he was downtown.

Blakely Koob and her telltale fingers. Photo courtesy of Koob family.

I have attached a picture that I snapped while the children were talking with Santa. If you look closely at my daughter's fingers, you will see something pretty amusing. I can only assume that is when Santa was asking her if she had been a good girl that year!

While there are many things that have changed since I was a child, it means a lot to know that some things, such as the simple act of visiting Santa, remain the same."

This is but a small sampling of the depth of feeling that Legendary Santa's "babies" of all ages have for him. But one more story speaks to the importance of Legendary Santa in the lives of his followers… past, present and future.

"I am pregnant with my first child…due June 2011," Amber Singh explained. This child will be the third generation of Williamsons (my maiden name) to visit Legendary Santa (we call him the "real" Santa). My father and I both visited him when he was still in Miller & Rhoads downtown. We always went to the tea, and ate Reindeer Cake, visited Bruce the Spruce, and I always bought my Christmas presents at the little Fawn Shop. I can't wait for this child to arrive so that we can have photos of three generations of children sitting on the "real" Santa's lap. And how special it will be that this child's first Christmas with Legendary Santa will be on the 75th anniversary!

I always encourage my friends who have moved to Richmond from outside the area to take their children to see Legendary Santa because of the amazing experience it is for children, and the wonderful tradition it makes."

16

LEGENDARY SANTA'S STORIES FROM THE CHAIR

Some Special Memories

Hermie Sadler

HERMIE SADLER, NASCAR driver from Emporia: "We've been going to see Legendary Santa as long as I can remember. And by we, I mean my whole family – my brother Elliott, my Mom and Dad, grandparents, aunts, uncles, cousins. Sometimes there would be twenty to thirty of us, driving from Emporia to Richmond. My wife, Angie, used to do the same thing with her family. Now we take our girls – Cora, Halie, and Naomi. We go every year and Cora says she wants to be a Snow Queen one day."

NASCAR stars Elliott and Hermie Sadler still are not too big to sit in Santa's lap. Photo courtesy of Angie Sadler.

Hermie Sadler and his wife Angie have been coming from Emporia to see Santa since they were children. Photo courtesy of Angie Sadler.

Bill Bevins

BILL BEVINS, host of the Lite 98 Morning Show. "In my memory, I can see my big sisters and myself at Miller & Rhoads. Unfortunately, I can't seem to be able to locate the photos but the image in black and white is clear….biggest sister, Susan, helping Drucilla and Billy up to the big guy's knee. It was one half of the twice a year trips downtown, for the Bevins kids.

Years later my wife, Debbie, and I took our twin boys, Jacob and Austin, to see Legendary Santa. It was one of the last years in the old building. By their last visit, they had visited Santa at the Richmond Convention Center and finally, at the Children's Museum of Richmond. Through it all, the magic that all of us witnessed was still just as evident as it was light-years ago, when big Sis put me on that very special knee."

Austin and Jacob Bevins

LEGENDARY SANTA'S STORIES FROM THE CHAIR

Illustrator Thomas Nast created what became the definitive artistic portrait of Santa Claus. Borrowing liberally from Clement C. Moore's written imagery in "The Night before Christmas" poem, Nast depicted Santa as a rotund, cheerful, white-bearded figure, attired in a red suit trimmed with white fur and carrying a sack bulging with toys. He first drew Santa for Harper's Weekly in 1863, during the Civil War, actually as a propaganda piece for the North. He continued to draw Santa for the magazine's Christmas editions until 1886. Nast has also been credited with creating the North Pole workshop, elves and Mrs. Claus.

Christmas parade photo courtesy of Jeff Marks.

LEGENDARY SANTA'S STORIES FROM THE CHAIR

Santa Claus Is Coming To Town

In the 75 years since Legendary Santa first came to Richmond, many things have changed. The city has changed and his location has changed, a number of times. But one thing has remained constant and enduring. The affection that Richmonders have demonstrated for this beloved figure has never changed, nor has his affection for them. To provide a framework for the memories and anecdotes collected for this book, here is a timeline of when Legendary Santa came to town.

"I had no idea when I first visited here in 1936, that I would make it my home for the next 75 years," Santa laughed, as he took a break during a busy day in Santa Land at the Children's Museum. "I had been invited to visit the toy department of Miller & Rhoads, which really seemed to be making a name for itself as one of the finest department stores in the South. In fact, they had celebrated their 50th anniversary the year before."

When Legendary Santa came to Richmond, the country was still in the grip of the Great Depression. However, Richmond fared better than many cities due to its then-strong tobacco industry and a diverse economy. Miller & Rhoads, which occupied almost a full city block along Grace Street, was called the centerpiece of "Richmond's Fifth Avenue." It maintained a friendly retail rivalry with another downtown landmark, Thalhimers.

Miller & Rhoads was a linchpin of Richmond's "Fifth Avenue." Photo courtesy of the Valentine Richmond History Center.

LEGENDARY SANTA'S STORIES FROM THE CHAIR

Holiday shoppers thronged the streets near Miller & Rhoads. Circa 1930s.

At Christmastime, the store brought a touch of New York sophistication to the Richmond streetscape, with elaborately decorated windows rivaling those of Macy's and other famous retailers. Though purse strings were tight, shoppers flocked in droves to marvel at the themed displays such as "The Night Before Christmas," Richmond trains, the Nativity, and many more. As if that wasn't enough to entice them into the store, they could visit Miller & Rhoads' honored guest, Legendary Santa, "the Real Santa," in the toy department.

Webster S. Rhoads, Jr. wrote in 1960 as Miller & Rhoads celebrated its 75th anniversary, that "The strangest institutional program we ever undertook was a Santa Claus. Christmas had always been a big thing at the store, but our Santa Clauses had been of the conventional variety." Of course, all of that changed when Legendary Santa came to town.

The Miller & Rhoads windows added to the holiday magic of downtown Richmond. Photo courtesy of the Valentine Richmond History Center.

LEGENDARY SANTA'S STORIES FROM THE CHAIR

"In 1942, over 15,000 people came to see me at Miller & Rhoads," Santa marveled. "This convinced the store to build a 'Santa Wonderland' on the seventh floor in the Old Dominion Room."

The look of the set that was created has remained very similar over the decades. The centerpiece, of course, was the fireplace and chimney where Santa made his much-anticipated entrance. Stockings were hung with care on the mantel. At one point, elegant candelabra decorated the mantel. Later a mantel clock was placed in the center with its hands at exactly five minutes to twelve. Santa's ornate gilded chair always commanded a regal position by the fireplace. A twinkling Christmas tree, bedecked with ornaments, shimmering tinsel and tiny lights flanked the chair.

The third floor also abounded with holiday activity. The Fawn Shop, located in the children's department, was designed just for kids so they could buy Christmas gifts all by themselves (with a little help from Miller & Rhoads employees.) The shop was child-sized and so were the prices of the items to accommodate little budgets.

Bruce the Spruce merrily reigned over the children's department. The talking Christmas Tree regaled his audiences with humorous observations about every passerby and his own celebrity status. Often he would burst into song but scramble the lyrics. "Let's sing!" he would exhort the kids gathered around him. "Rudolph the red-nosed possum…." "Noooo!" the kids shouted back, aghast at his mistake. "Rudolph the red-nosed reindeer!"

Santa and his friends became so successful that the company began doing commercials with the tagline "Miller & Rhoads - Where Christmas is a Legend."

Milton Burke, the store's long-time display coordinator, was responsible for seeing that Santa Land was ready for the thousands of visitors that came every December. "No two days were alike in my forty-four years," Burke laughed.

Angie Grooms Randolph worked in Santa Land for nineteen years as a cashier. It was a part-time job, from Thanksgiving to Christmas Eve, that gave her permanent memories.

The talking Christmas tree, Bruce the Spruce, merrily reigned over the childrens' department at Miller & Rhoads. Photo courtesy of the Richmond Times-Dispatch.

LEGENDARY SANTA'S STORIES FROM THE CHAIR

Santa comes down the chimney with an arm full of toys. Photo courtesy of Valentine Richmond History Center.

"I was the last person that you would see when you purchased your Santa photo," she explained. And from her vantage point, she saw a lot.

"I remember seeing people waiting in line for three and four hours to see Santa," she said. "One time there was so much overflow on the seventh floor that we had to move people to another floor."

"I have so many special memories," she said. "I would see the same children with their families, year after year. I could look forward to seeing the same families time after time."

Often the mothers in line would slip Angie their children's Christmas lists for her to give to Santa. However, she did not have much of an opportunity to talk with Santa because they were all so busy.

"I didn't even see him until the end of the evening, about 9:00 p.m.," she said.

When she did get a chance to see Santa, he knew her name, too.

"He would see me and call out 'Hey Angie how are you doing!'" she laughed. "Once I saw him at the Governor's Mansion for the Christmas Tree lighting and he just hugged me."

"I think Legendary Santa is so important because families need traditions," she noted. She said she always liked to hear folks say in Santa Land, "See you next year!"

People would wait in line for hours to see Legendary Santa. Photo courtesy of Valentine Richmond History Center. Circa 1950s.

24

LEGENDARY SANTA'S STORIES FROM THE CHAIR

End of an Era

At 8:00 a.m. on the day after Thanksgiving in 1989, hundreds of people waited in lines that stretched around the sixth and seventh floors at Miller & Rhoads. They came to see their beloved Legendary Santa for the last time in the grand old store, which was going out of business after 105 years.

Katherine Hockaday, age 79, of Yorktown, told the Richmond Times-Dispatch, " I've been coming here for forty years. I want to have my picture made with Legendary Santa."

Her daughter, Peggy Rich, of Virginia Beach, said, "It's not Christmas unless I come up here. There's nothing like it. No other store creates the magic."

Over 75,000 people reportedly flocked to see Legendary Santa in the five weeks from Thanksgiving to Christmas Eve that year, more than triple the usual number.

Santa Land was packed on Christmas Eve as Legendary Santa bid his final farewell to the audience. Many families who had been coming for years were there, as were Santa Land staff and Miller & Rhoads officials. It was an emotional moment for all assembled, and more than a few tears were shed.

Santa, maintaining his composure, told the children, "Now if I have time, when I come to your house tonight, I'll come into your room. In the morning you'll know I was there because I will leave a sooty fingerprint on your forehead."

He made no mention of the store's closing as he wished everyone a Merry Christmas and stooped down to get in the chimney. The crowd gasped as they always did as he rose up into the chimney, his big black boots dangling for a moment before they vanished. Children near the stage cried out: "We love you Santa!"

The Snow Queen, standing by the fireplace, said "And I heard him exclaim as he flew out of sight…." To the sound of sleigh bells growing fainter in the distance, Santa answered: "Merry Christmas to all and to all a good night!"

A memorable era for Legendary Santa and Richmond was over. For awhile, things were in limbo.

"After Miller & Rhoads closed its doors, the newspaper reported that I was 'homeless'," said Legendary Santa. "Of course I still had my home at the North Pole!" he laughed. "You know, I was not any sadder on that last day at Miller & Rhoads than we usually are in Santa Land at the end of a season. I knew it was my last day there, but not my last day in Richmond. I was not planning to leave Richmond!"

Likewise, the Richmond community was determined to carry on the cherished tradition of Legendary Santa. Wheels were in motion and in May of 1990, Thalhimers, the friendly retail rival of

LEGENDARY SANTA'S STORIES FROM THE CHAIR

Miller & Rhoads, announced that it would be Santa's new home. The store stayed true to the original Santa Land program and also added new elements such as the lovable Snow Bear and talented performers from the Theatre IV children's troupe.

Sadly, Thalhimers met the same fate as Miller & Rhoads as shoppers continued to desert downtown stores for shiny new suburban malls. This meant Legendary Santa would have to move again. Undaunted, Santa and his legions of supporters took it in stride.

"I was so touched by how hard Richmonders were fighting to keep this tradition alive," Santa said. "Many people worked very hard to make sure Legendary Santa still had a home here."

In July 1991, the Times Dispatch reported that Legendary Santa would be back in the old Miller & Rhoads building on the first floor. His visitors would come in through the Sixth Street Marketplace. This was a "festival marketplace," a downtown revitalization project featuring specialty shops and kiosks, restaurants, a food court and other trendy attractions.

This time his host was Downtown Presents, the city's promotional arm. "I'm excited that Santa's coming home," said Nina Abady, executive director at the time. "It has meant so much to generations of Richmonders to have Santa downtown."

"Old Santa is very happy to be in downtown Richmond," Legendary Santa concurred. Back in Santa Land, he was reunited with Bruce the Spruce, the talking and singing Christmas tree that had delighted children in the toy department at Miller & Rhoads. Kids could also enjoy free train rides around Festival Park when they came to see Santa.

After the Thalhimers building was vacated, Santa moved back there again. It was now called Theatre Square. Visitors entered via the second floor of Sixth Street Marketplace. Downtown Presents enthusiastically promoted Legendary Santa as the centerpiece of the city's seasonal festivities, with themes such as "Reindeer Days – Downtown Richmond's Spectacular Holiday Celebration!" Legendary Santa's arrival, the Grand Illumination at the James Center, the Ukrops/Jaycees Christmas Parade, the Nutcracker Ballet and a host of holiday festivities enticed visitors to downtown Richmond. The "Reindeer Express" decorated trolleys transported weekend shoppers to various points of interest. Children could visit Legendary Santa in "the classic Santaland at Theatre Square" and even have breakfast or lunch with him on the Sixth Street Marketplace bridge for $4.50 per ticket.

The Children's Museum of Richmond, then called the Richmond Children's Museum, even played a role in Reindeer Days. They hosted a "Snow Crystal Castle and Wonderland Workshop" in Shockoe Slip. It featured stage performances, holiday craft-making, storytelling and visits with holiday characters. The Reindeer Express connected the castle with the museum's original location on Navy Hill Drive near the Medical College of Virginia.

In 2002, Santa moved one more time in downtown Richmond, making his new holiday headquarters the Richmond Convention Center.

LEGENDARY SANTA'S STORIES FROM THE CHAIR

"The moving to different locations was not hard on me," Santa noted. "People are so wonderful. They continued to come from all over, no matter where we were!"

K Alferio, then executive director of Downtown Presents, which later became City Celebrations, agreed, "Wherever Legendary Santa was, people would follow. It is a testament to the community and the people who have produced the program. Few things could have withstood all that Santa went through, but all the organizations understood how important this was."

Alferio had a special affinity for Legendary Santa, as she had worked with a Santa program in Atlanta. Later her own daughter would be a Snow Queen.

She emphasized that even though his location changed, the tradition remained the same. "We were very careful to keep the tradition in the right direction. That meant being very selective about other events Legendary Santa participated in, such as the Jaycees/Ukrops Christmas Parade. You don't want to overdo the magic."

From Richmond Times-Dispatch, November 23, 1994.

In 2005, City Celebrations and the Children's Museum of Richmond announced that the museum would be the new and permanent home of Legendary Santa. Alferio confessed to having mixed emotions about Santa's departure.

"It had been difficult not owning the space for him at the Convention Center and the program really needed a sense of permanency," she said. "It was an honor to be a steward of it and my wish is that Legendary Santa will continue for another seventy-five years!"

On September 22, 2005, the Children's Museum of Richmond (CMoR) transformed into a winter wonderland complete with falling snow and dancing elves as it welcomed Legendary Santa. The jolly old elf made a grand entrance in an 18-wheeler moving van.

All the familiar fixtures of Santa Land were in place inside the museum: Santa's gilded chair, the fireplace and chimney, the mantel clock, the Christmas tree. The Snow Queen was there along with Santa's newest helper - a big, cuddly red dinosaur named Seymour, the CMoR mascot.

The merry sound of Christmas carols filled the air, played on the keyboard by Debo Dabney, the talented pianist who performed at the Santa events in the Miller & Rhoads Tea Room after the beloved organist Eddie Weaver retired. At the reception, all the guests enjoyed – what else – Reindeer Cake!

LEGENDARY SANTA'S STORIES FROM THE CHAIR

Museum officials expressed their excitement of being able to offer a convenient location in the city, with free parking and a variety of activities at the museum to entertain the children waiting in line to see Santa. The museum was also the new home of the Genworth Financial Holiday Village, which presented an array of holiday cultural traditions.

K Alferio said at the ceremony, "In terms of the audience, the location and the mission, there could be no better place for Legendary Santa than the Children's Museum of Richmond."

Legendary Santa, who was accompanied by the Snow Queen, said, "I am looking forward to settling in my new home at the Children's Museum and greeting all the boys and girls soon."

After seventy-five years and several moves, many people have wondered…of all the places he could have chosen, why did Legendary Santa pick Richmond, Virginia?

"I was so impressed with the atmosphere that they established because it was so child-centered and friendly," Santa said. "The children and parents in Richmond were the ones who made me want to come every year. They made it feel like home from the very start. The people here are gracious, kind and appreciative. The tradition, love of children and strong values of the folks in Richmond have made it one of my favorite places every year. Richmond will always be my home away from home."

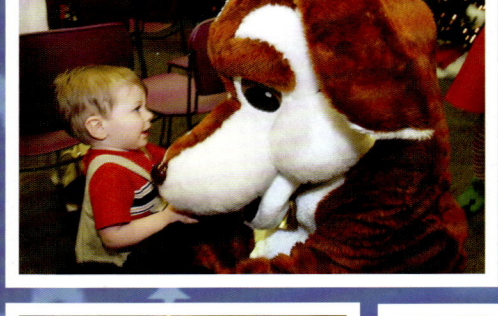

The Children's Museum of Richmond happily welcomed Legendary Santa to his new permanent home in 2005.

LEGENDARY SANTA'S STORIES FROM THE CHAIR

Legendary Santa takes his job so seriously that he has taken an oath of service. The helpers who work at department stores, the malls, parades, etc. also follow this creed.

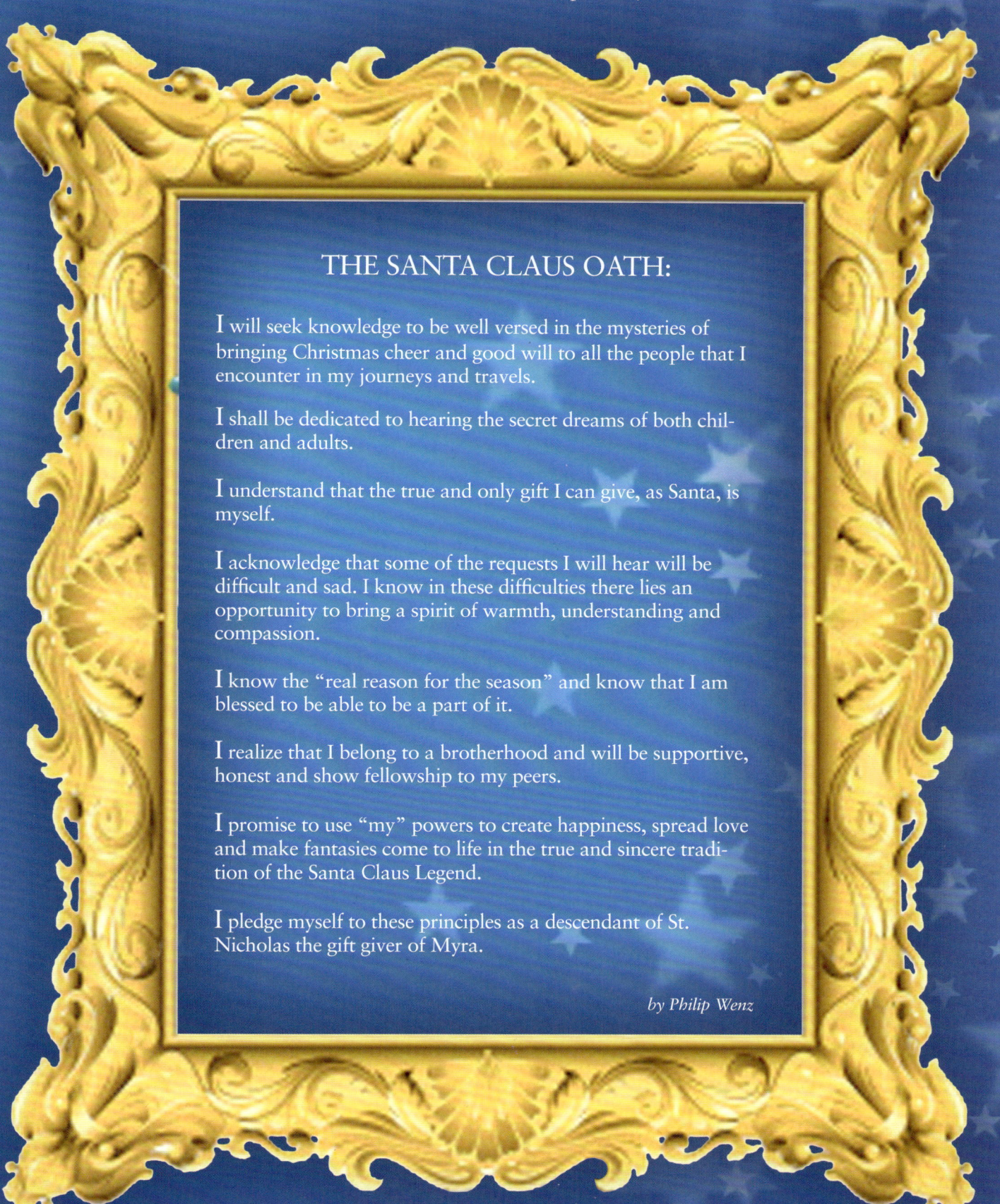

THE SANTA CLAUS OATH:

I will seek knowledge to be well versed in the mysteries of bringing Christmas cheer and good will to all the people that I encounter in my journeys and travels.

I shall be dedicated to hearing the secret dreams of both children and adults.

I understand that the true and only gift I can give, as Santa, is myself.

I acknowledge that some of the requests I will hear will be difficult and sad. I know in these difficulties there lies an opportunity to bring a spirit of warmth, understanding and compassion.

I know the "real reason for the season" and know that I am blessed to be able to be a part of it.

I realize that I belong to a brotherhood and will be supportive, honest and show fellowship to my peers.

I promise to use "my" powers to create happiness, spread love and make fantasies come to life in the true and sincere tradition of the Santa Claus Legend.

I pledge myself to these principles as a descendant of St. Nicholas the gift giver of Myra.

by Philip Wenz

LEGENDARY SANTA'S STORIES FROM THE CHAIR

MEMORIES OF DOWNTOWN RICHMOND AT CHRISTMASTIME

Every year in my hometown of Richmond, VA, from my mother's post-WWII childhood through my own youth, Legendary Santa came to Miller & Rhoads department store in the heart of downtown. The entire city was resplendent in Christmas decor. There were extravagant street-front holiday window displays. There was Bruce the Spruce, the "live" Christmas tree, who never ceased to fascinate me despite my dad's annual explanation as to the logistics behind a talking tree. And the entire 7th floor of Miller & Rhoads, normally vacant storage space, was transformed into a magic wonderland called "Santa Land." This was downtown Richmond in its prime. And every year we were there to experience it.

Because the lines were so long for the Legendary Santa on weekends, my parents pulled my younger brother and me out of school on a December afternoon each year. Dressed in our Sunday best, we'd head downtown as a family. We'd watch with awe as Santa came down the chimney and took his place on his gilded chair. Then we'd wait (sometimes not so patiently) in line for our turn to sit on his lap. First, we'd chat with his Snow Queen. Then we'd visit with Santa himself and tick off each item on our Christmas list. Finally, we had our picture taken by an elf. My mom still has every picture we ever took with Santa Claus. (from Kristin Harris Alexander of the blog What She Said at www.shesaid.us.)

❄

Miller & Rhoads had the most beautiful windows at Christmas, and Thalhimers was next. Other shops along the streets decorated their windows but they never came close to the two big stores. On the Grace Street side of the stores, people would spend hours on a nice day standing at the windows and walking up and down the streets.

Christmas music was piped out onto the streets around Miller & Rhoads and Thalhimers. Some of the windows were full of animated people and things, especially Miller & Rhoads' windows. Their big window at the corner of 6th and Grace, which faced both streets, always had Santa's workshop and it was beautiful. It truly looked like the North Pole and was a beehive of activity. There was so much to see and so such continuous activity one could stand there for an hour. Elves were making things, painting, carrying, etc. ... all kinds of things going on and continuous movement.

LEGENDARY SANTA'S STORIES FROM THE CHAIR

It was absolutely fascinating because at that time, not many people had seen that sort of thing. Miller & Rhoads' window facing 5th Street and Grace Street was full of trains and that, too, was wonderful! We loved watching all of those trains going in every direction - and I still love trains.

Downtown Richmond was beautiful in those days and was absolutely fantastic at Christmas time! We would dress up, with our hats and gloves, and go downtown on Saturdays. We would spend the whole day shopping and having lunch, then would head home about 4 o'clock….We did not have much money but those were the best years of my life! (from Lynn Mitchell at http://swac-girl.blogspot.com)

The elaborately decorated windows of Miller & Rhoads enchanted onlookers with their various themes. Photo courtesy of Valentine Richmond History Center.

Santa Land decorations. Photo courtesy of the Cobb family.

31

Story excerpted with permission of Style Magazine.

Christmas Memories
Thalhimers 1992

by Elizabeth Thalhimer Smartt

My vision blurs with tears and my heartbeat quickens as I hurry down Sixth Street, alone, towards the familiar building. Fifteen years ago, I held my little sisters' hands as we gleefully skipped down the same sidewalk in our shiny Mary Janes, matching smocked dresses and velvet-collared winter coats. Only surpassed in excitement by Christmas morning itself, our annual downtown visit to see Santa marked the highlight of each holiday season. And I know I'm not the only Richmonder with cherished memories of those glorious days.

I prepare myself for the inevitable realization that this visit will be different from those of my childhood. It's my first visit back to the Thalhimers flagship store since it closed in 1992, and it may well be the last. It's Santa's final year at the downtown Thalhimers and I am going to interview him for Style Magazine.

The windows that once held animated holiday characters frolicking around little winterscapes are now empty. The front doors that used to welcome streams of customers are chained shut. The sign that read "Thalhimers" now reads…nothing. My heart aches as I recall the vibrant scene that once graced this desolate place. It used to be so different here. I am afraid I might cry.

And once I see Santa Land I do cry, but not out of sorrow. I cry because two little girls in Mary Janes and red velveteen dresses boisterously skip past me, holding hands. They spot Santa, and their golden ringlets bounce as they dash to meet him. Laughter reverberates throughout the festively decorated room while hundreds upon hundreds of children of all ages weave their way towards the Snow Queen, the Elf, and, finally, the Legendary Santa Claus. Forgetting to acknowledge that I'm once again setting foot in the beloved Thalhimers of old, I am magically drawn into the spirited scene.

Santa still sits in his majestic green velvet and gold trimmed armchair in front of the famous chimney that he comes down every morning. Snowflakes hang from the ceiling, holly and red bows garnish the mantelpiece, and, to my delight, familiar animated bears and playful penguins from the Santa Land of my memories keep the children entertained.

I begin to notice that not all adults in attendance are accompanied by little ones. Elderly couples meander around the enchanted room. Twenty-somethings stop by to catch a glimpse of the "Real Santa." Two couples, who look to be in their mid-forties, greet each other at the Santa Land entrance. One visitor tells me that no matter where Legendary Santa ends up, she will visit him.

After all of the visitors have left for the day, it's my turn to sit on Santa's knee. "I've been downtown for thirty-six years. Half of the moms and dads who come in here sat on my knee when they were kids," Santa tells me. "I have so many fond memories of seeing those boys and girls here, and will stay downtown as long as I can." Then, before I can argue otherwise, we are immortalized by the click of a camera.

And, in that instant, I smile as big as I did when I was a little girl.

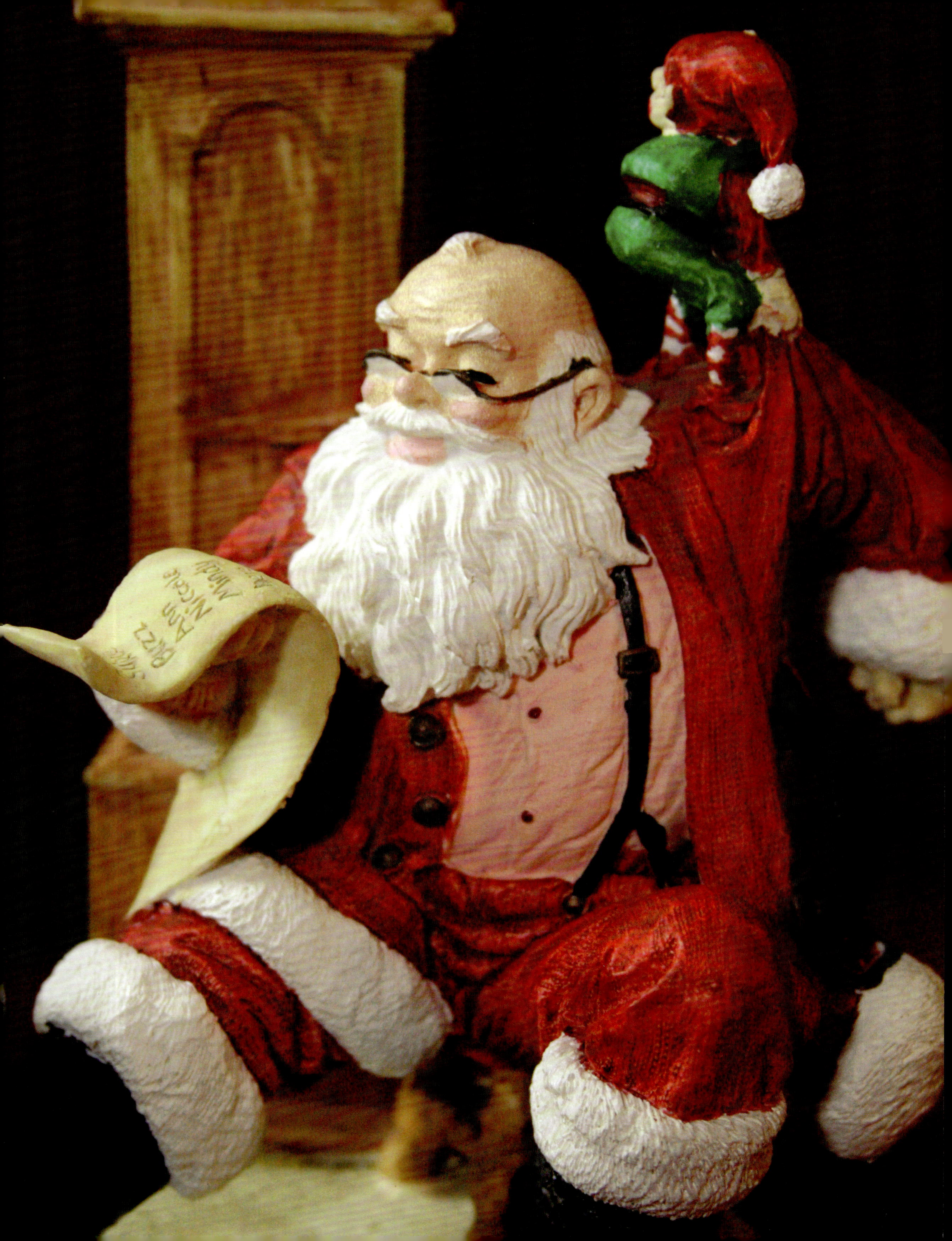
Buzz
Ann
Nicole
Mindy

LEGENDARY SANTA'S STORIES FROM THE CHAIR

Making a List and Checking It Twice

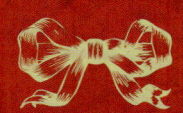

LOCATION: THE CHILDREN'S MUSEUM OF RICHMOND, ANYTIME BETWEEN THE DAY AFTER THANKSGIVING AND THE AFTERNOON OF CHRISTMAS EVE…

"Now have you been thinking of what you want for Christmas?" Legendary Santa asks after making his ceremonial descent down the chimney to the twinkling stage of Santa Land. The excited youngsters waiting in line answer him with a resounding YES!

"And have you been good this year?" Santa inquires with a merry wink.

"YES!" repeats the emphatic chorus of young voices.

Santa surveys the sea of expectant faces before him, as he has countless times before. Even with today's casual dress code, most of the young children are dressed in their holiday finest. Little girls are wearing red and black dresses with velvet boleros, black patent leather shoes, burgundy dresses with shimmering sequins, Mary Jane shoes with rhinestone buckles, green velvet dresses, red plaid skirts, red Christmas sweaters with appliquéd angels, matching bows in their hair, some carrying their dolls in matching outfits. The boys look freshly scrubbed, their hair neatly combed, wearing bowties and vests, jaunty plaid caps, grownup-looking blazers and dress shirts, pressed khakis and penny loafers.

In a beloved ritual that has changed little over the decades, Santa settles himself on the green velvet cushion of his gilded throne and introduces the lovely Snow Queen. She comes onstage and walks to her shimmering chair as he remarks, "Now isn't she beautiful? She has such a beautiful smile. Old Santa loves smiles."

LEGENDARY SANTA'S STORIES FROM THE CHAIR

Next he asks the Elf to bring him his mirror and comb so he can put the finishing touches on his snowy beard and flowing locks.

At last, he's ready! The first children in line walk up the steps to the stage and talk with the Snow Queen, whose kind smile and gentle demeanor immediately put them at ease. Then as only Legendary Santa can do, he calls the children by name, jovially beckoning them to "Come on over!"

Some kids bound across the stage right into Santa's arms. Some walk over shyly, with a little encouragement from Mom and Dad, who quickly scurry to the sidelines to take photos or videotape the big event. Often, the enormity of the moment overwhelms some youngsters. Those who were chattering in line only minutes earlier suddenly lose the power of speech when Santa shows them the microphone. After carefully preparing their Christmas list for months, they can only nod mutely as Santa asks them if they know what they want him to bring.

Most of them, however, are only too happy to regale Legendary Santa with the litany of presents they want for Christmas. And just in case he doesn't commit it all to memory, they can conveniently leave copies of their lists with the Elf, who sits near Santa's chair. At the end of the season, after over 25,000 visitors have passed through Santa Land at the Children's Museum, the collected lists fill up several large bags. Santa, of course, takes these back to the North Pole for handy reference.

And what lists they are! Some are scribbled in crayon on notebook paper; many are written on paper printed with holiday designs. Children bring lists decorated with their own drawings of Santa, his reindeer, Christmas trees and snowmen. Many cut out pictures of the toys or items they want and glue them to their lists; others create very thorough documents on their computers, complete with the images and prices for each desired item and where they can be purchased!

"I want to share some of the more recent lists for this book," Legendary Santa said. "You will be amazed at some of the things the children ask for," he laughed. "Then I want to tell you about some of the favorite toys the children have requested over the past 75 years."

"In 2010, children (young and obviously not so young) asked for all sorts of things," Santa said. "They wanted everything from beef jerky to a Dairy Queen Blizzard Maker, from Easy Bake Ovens to electric guitars to electric train sets, and from duct tape to a Visa debit card! Here are some more items:"

LEGENDARY SANTA'S STORIES FROM THE CHAIR

What childen asked for in 2010.

A door bell for their room
A Harley Davidson
Tickets to a Phillies game
Lego Space Police
Pillow Pets
A Learner's permit
A bank to save money
Laptops
Xbox 360
Digital cameras
Crayola Glow Station
Rocket Pogo Stick
Hula Hoops
American Girl dolls
DVD players
Wireless mic and stand and headset
Flip video camera
Cell phones
IPads
IPods
Wii
Easy Bake Oven
Play-Doh
Stinky the Garbage Truck
"the little guy that pees"
A Teddy bear made by an elf
Silly Bandz
Slinky
New samba shoes
Tickets to a Redskins game
Nerf guns
Smith & Wesson M3000 Chief special airsoft gun
A camo hunting belt, shotgun and side knife
Hip waders, fly tying kit, tackle box
A "vroom-vroom"
New bow and arrow set
Skateboards
A bell from Santa's "slaiye"
A robot that can do my homework and play with me
A Mustang car
Barbie Escalade
ZuZu pets

LEGENDARY SANTA'S STORIES FROM THE CHAIR

"Often the children were very specific about the brands they preferred. Advertisers will love to hear that!" Santa noted. "They want Nike shoes, Polo shirts, UGG boots, Mac Book Pro, Vera Bradley bags, North Face jackets, Oakley sunglasses, a Rolex watch and Aeropostale, Hollister and Abercrombie clothes."

"Many of them asked for gift cards from their favorite retailers," Santa said. "They like Macy's, Starbucks, Old Navy, Target, Best Buy and Shoe Carnival, to name a few."

"Pets are also popular. The letters ranged from general requests to quite detailed," said Santa.

"Someone wrote me asking for a live snake. Another child wanted a dog that eats and poops. I don't know if they meant a real dog or a toy. Here are some other pets:"

An actual girl piglet
An allergy-free real puppy
A real girl puppy
A real live horse
An English Bulldog

A Yorkie
A Chocolate Lab
A King Charles Spaniel
A Coccer (Cocker) Spaniel
A Goldendoodle

"And a young girl asked for a horse that lives down the road at a neighbor's house along with a new bridle and blanket. I don't know how the neighbor felt about that!" Santa said.

I even had one boy ask me for an elephant. I asked him if he could think of anything else and he said 'What else you got?'"

Santa pointed out that sometimes the requests are for items other than toys or games.

38

LEGENDARY SANTA'S STORIES FROM THE CHAIR

"Children will ask me to make it snow all week!" Santa laughed. "They say they want to see Rudolph or Dancer or the other reindeer. They want to have an elf come to their house."

He said that letter-writers ask such things as:

"I want to become famous!"

"I want my voice to be amazing!"

"I want a bunch of surprises but nothing in particular, please."

"Please put anything that fits in my stocking."

"Can you send me a video of you at your workshop?"

"We want a UNC championship!"

"My Dad would like a Cowboys football. He deserves it because he is the best dad ever!"

"I want a billion dollars and I will be good for the rest of my life!"

LEGENDARY SANTA'S STORIES FROM THE CHAIR

"I do get some interesting questions in these letters," he said. "Children want to know how do I fit in their chimney; is my toy sack brown or red; or can I give them one of my hats?"

"Some children add additional information in their letters, which they, no doubt, hope will be helpful to me," Santa laughed. "Here are some samples:"

"I have been good for the most part."

"I know I'm not going to get all of this."

"You are welcome to bring anything else you think I would like."

"I've been an excellent little boy this year."

"I'm a good boy but need to sleep in my big boy bed." (in Mom's handwriting)

"I've been a good girl, got all A's and B's."

"I've been a good boy, but not perfect. I always get green faces in kindergarten."

"I might have been a little bad this year but I still believe in joy, happiness and you. "

"I've been good everywhere. I haven't hit anybody."

"We have no chimney so feel free to use the front door."

"I still believe."

Santa noted that, while children of the 21st century often want expensive, sophisticated items for Christmas such as laptops and cell phones, they also ask for toys which have been around for generations. He reminisced about toy fads he has seen come and go and come again over the years.

"When children first started visiting me at Miller & Rhoads in 1936, the nation was still trying to climb out of the Great Depression," Santa said.

"Toys were simple and inexpensive. Back then, the boys and girls wanted things like pogo sticks, Raggedy Ann dolls and Superman comic books," said Santa. "Board games were popular then, especially Monopoly, which had just come out. "

40

LEGENDARY SANTA'S STORIES FROM THE CHAIR

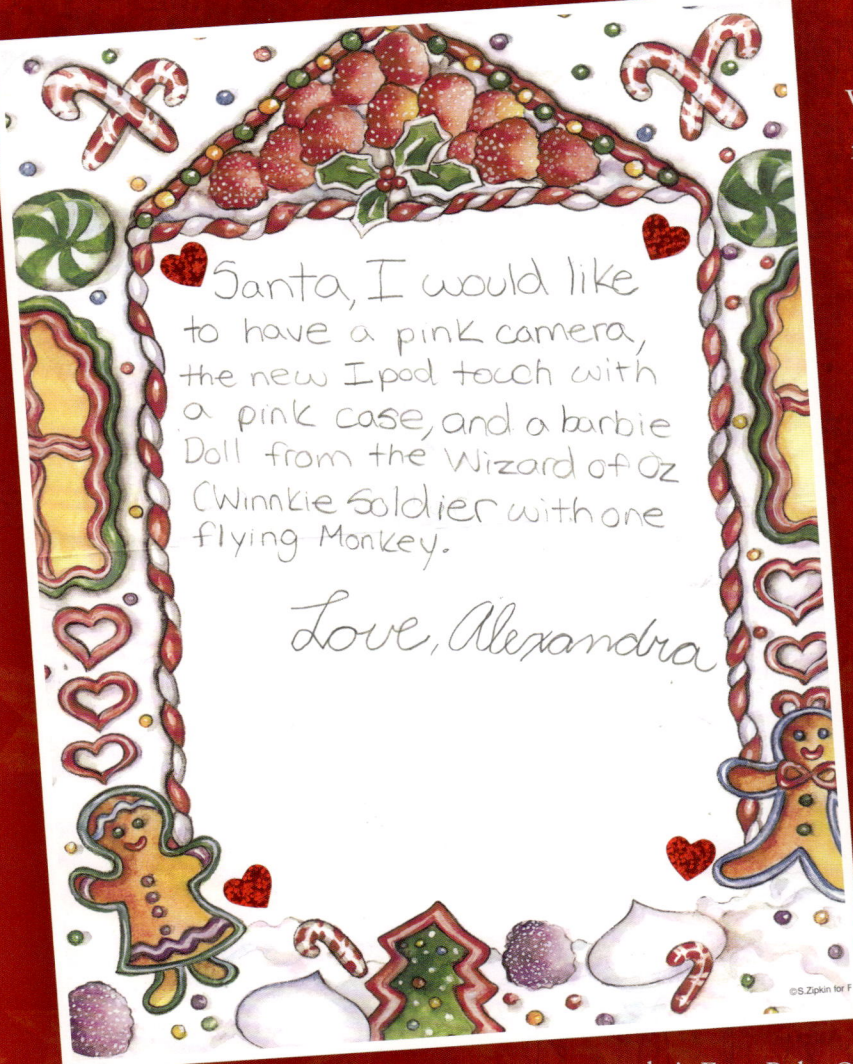

> Santa, I would like to have a pink camera, the new Ipod touch with a pink case, and a barbie Doll from the Wizard of Oz (Winnkie Soldier with one flying Monkey.
>
> Love, Alexandra

In the 1940s, America was fighting World War II but that didn't stop children from wanting toys or Santa from bringing them.

"Candy Land and Chutes and Ladders came out in the 1940s and everyone wanted those," Santa said. "Tonka trucks and model airplanes were big hits with the boys."

The 1950s brought an avalanche of new toys for the post-war phenomenon of the "baby boomer generation."

Legendary Santa noted, "My sleigh was full of Mr. Potato Heads, Hula Hoops, Silly Putty, Play-Doh, Barbie dolls, Legos, Lincoln Logs, TinkerToys, Yo-Yos and Slinkys!"

In the 1960s, little girls could "cook" just like their moms with their Easy-Bake Ovens. Boys could indulge their military fantasies with the action figure of G.I. Joe, which came out prior to the Vietnam War.

"Boys and girls alike loved the Etch-A-Sketch," Santa recalled. "And everyone got tangled up with the new party game Twister!"

"In the 1970s, the latest craze was the Rubik's Cube," said Santa. "Skateboards came out and then turned into a real sport. The 70s are when the electronic games started to emerge with the Atari system and Pong." Other popular toys were Matchbox cars, dolls named Crissy and Velvet, Hungry Hungry Hippos, Star Wars action figures and NERF balls.

"The 1980s gave me a fit with the Cabbage Patch dolls," Santa laughed. "There was a shortage and my elves were working overtime to fill all the orders!"

Two new board games, Trivial Pursuit and Pictionary, hit the market, as did My Little Pony, Care Bears, Transformers and the wildly-in-demand Teenage Mutant Ninja Turtles.

The 1990s saw a repeat of the Cabbage Patch Doll problem.

LEGENDARY SANTA'S STORIES FROM THE CHAIR

"That's when Tickle Me Elmo also was in short supply," said Santa. "I didn't think I'd have that problem again so soon!"

The talking Furbys created a sensation during the decade, which also saw Beanie Babies, the Nintendo Game Boy, Power Rangers and Pokemon, to name a few.

Yet for all the typical preoccupation with the latest and greatest toys, clothes, electronics, pets or other gifts, many young letter-writers display an innate understanding of the true spirit of Christmas and genuine concern for their beloved Legendary Santa.

"These are the letters that always get to me," said Santa. Here is a sampling of what is on the minds of children besides material things:

"First of all, I want to make sure that you don't spend too much time on my presents. I want to make sure you give other kids toys and plenty of other things. Thanks for all you do!"

"Thank you for all you give me and others. I hope you have a good trip around the world."

"I wish they would bring all the soldiers home from Iraq so Daddy won't ever have to go again."

"I wish that all of Haiti's problems are solved."

"Please help North and South Korea settle their differences peacefully."

"World peace would be nice."

"Blessings of good health."

"I'd like to have a restaurant dinner for Mom and Dad."

"I want a Happy New Year for my whole family."

"Thank you for letting me see you fly through the sky after church last Christmas. I hope that all of the houses that you go to on Christmas night have cookies."

"Thank you for the wonderful toys last year. Have a fun and safe trip. We love you."

"You are the best. I hope you have a jolly Christmas."

"Santa, you rock!"

"Thanks for being our Santa!"

"Happy Holidays! We like your beard!"

"Please tell all the reindeer and Mrs. Claus that I love them."

LEGENDARY SANTA'S STORIES FROM THE CHAIR

"I'd especially like to request that all the underprivileged children have their dreams come true. Have a wonderful and safe Christmas!"

And lastly, the request that lives in all the hearts of humankind:

"Santa, please bring peace and happiness for everybody in the world."

In 1821, a New York printer named William Gilley published a poem about a "Santeclaus" in a book entitled *"The Children's Friend."* The character dressed in fur and drove a sleigh pulled by one reindeer. The poem vividly describes what Santeclaus brought good little boys and girls, as well as what naughty children could expect to receive!

Old SANTECLAUS with much delight
His reindeer drives this frosty night,
O'er chimney-tops, and tracks of snow,
To bring his yearly gifts to you.

The steady friend of virtuous youth,
The friend of duty, and of truth,
Each Christmas eve he joys to come
Where love and peace have made their home.

Santeclaus, *"The Children's Friend"* 1821

Through many houses he has been,
And various beds and stockings seen;
Some, white as snow, and neatly mended,
Others, that seemed for pigs intended.

Where e'er I found good girls or boys,
That hated quarrels, strife and noise,
I left an apple, or a tart,
Or wooden gun, or painted cart.

To some I gave a pretty doll,
To some a peg-top, or a ball;
No crackers, cannons, squibs, or rockets,
To blow their eyes up, or their pockets.

No drums to stun their Mother's ear,
Nor swords to make their sisters fear;
But pretty books to store their mind
With knowledge of each various kind.

But where I found the children naughty,
In manners rude, in temper haughty,
Thankless to parents, liars, swearers,
Boxers, or cheats, or base tale-bearers,

I left a long, black, birchen rod,
Such as the dread command of God
Directs a Parent's hand to use
When virtue's path his sons refuse.

LEGENDARY SANTA'S STORIES FROM THE CHAIR

THE $19 DOLL

Legendary Santa shared this story of a little girl who desperately wanted a certain baby doll:

"Her name was Carolyn and she was seven years old. She had shown the doll to her mother at Miller & Rhoads and her mother was upset because the doll cost nineteen dollars. That doesn't sound like much today when children ask for I-Pads and video games, but at the time, it was a lot of money, especially for a single mom.

"Her mother was even more shocked when Carolyn told me exactly how much the doll cost, as it wasn't considered polite to discuss money with Santa! But I brought her the baby doll, which she promptly named Margaret for her mother.

"Years later, Carolyn wrote me to say that Margaret was the most-loved doll baby in all of baby doll land and that she became her own daughter's favorite doll. She said that 'Every time I unwrap her (the doll) I smile and remember that special day with the real Santa.'"

Every Boy Wants a Train

Paul Miller had a very vivid memory about wanting an electric train for Christmas.

"Every time a boy would tell Santa he wanted an electric train, Santa would belt out a very loud "Woo! Woo!" (like a train whistle). It was so loud you could hear it everywhere on the floor. The kids in line would hear this and ask for an electric train just so that they could hear Santa imitate the train whistle. It occurred to me years later that Miller & Rhoads was probably pushing electric train sales. It so happens I got one that year, one of my favorite Christmas gifts ever!"

1953 photo: Left to right: Paul Miller, his brother Joe on Santa's lap and a friend named Tommy Walsh.

Photo courtesy of Paul Miller

44

LEGENDARY SANTA'S STORIES FROM THE CHAIR

The Man Who Loved Santa Claus

On Christmas Eve, 1975, Jayne Hushen and her father Jack had some last minute shopping to do at Miller & Rhoads. He wanted to get a gift for Jayne and needed to go off on his own. They agreed to meet later at Santa Land at an agreed upon time.

Jayne finished up a little early and decided to go ahead up to the seventh floor to Santa Land. When she arrived, she saw the usual crowd of parents and children waiting in line to see Legendary Santa, just as she had done for many years. However, people were pointing and chuckling at something that Jayne couldn't see. Something was causing quite a stir in the room. Wanting to see what the excitement was, she edged around the crowd for a better look.

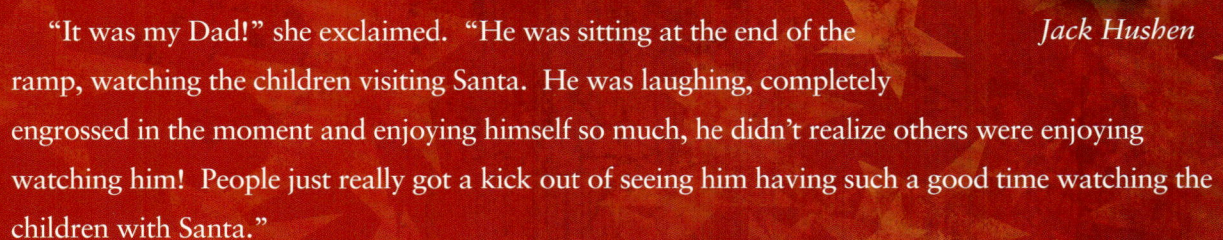

"It was my Dad!" she exclaimed. "He was sitting at the end of the ramp, watching the children visiting Santa. He was laughing, completely engrossed in the moment and enjoying himself so much, he didn't realize others were enjoying watching him! People just really got a kick out of seeing him having such a good time watching the children with Santa."

Jack Hushen

Jayne explained that because of their respective schedules, she and her Dad did not usually have a lot of time to spend together. "I thank God for this memory of my Dad because he passed away just weeks before the next Christmas. I will treasure that memory the rest of my life," she said.

Santa Works in Mysterious Ways

Cindy Harrison was coming down the escalator at Miller & Rhoads after visiting with Legendary Santa when she spied something she wanted for Christmas. It was a gigantic stuffed animal, a German Shepherd to be exact. It was within arm's reach, "so I just grabbed it," she said. Clutching her prize, Cindy followed her unsuspecting mother to the front door. The doorman politely stopped them and the German Shepherd remained in the store. However Cindy found him under the tree on Christmas Day.

One year Cindy and her mother returned from shopping to discover that someone had broken into their house and stolen all the Christmas presents. On Christmas Eve, Cindy's mother told her to go to sleep because Santa was coming. When she woke up Christmas Day, she had presents under the tree. More proof of the magic of Santa Claus!

Snow Queen Lisa Ramos with Legendary Santa. Photo courtesy of Lisa Ramos.

LEGENDARY SANTA'S STORIES FROM THE CHAIR

Favorite Memories from the Snow Queens

LOCATION: THE CHILDREN'S MUSEUM OF RICHMOND, CHRISTMAS 2010:

"Now here's the Snow Queen!" Legendary Santa exclaims as he settles into his great green velvet chair onstage in Santa Land after coming down the chimney. "Isn't she beautiful? Doesn't she have a beautiful smile?"

The Snow Queen walks across the stage, a vision in her shimmering white satin dress and sparkling tiara. Poised and graceful, she takes her place on her own throne which almost looks to be carved of ice and is embedded with tiny twinkling lights. But there is nothing icy in the Snow Queen's demeanor. She exudes warmth and friendliness. After all, she is the first one to greet the children before they visit with Legendary Santa.

Legendary Santa relies a great deal on his Snow Queen.

"Snow Queen sets the tone for each child's visit," said Legendary Santa. "She represents youth, beauty and kindness. Her ability to be charming and caring helps create the magic of Santa Land.

"Not only is she beautiful, but she has the right voice," Santa noted. "She speaks very clearly as she is talking to the children or their parents. She is a calming influence and helps things run smoothly."

Countless times a day, the Snow Queen says, "Now in just a minute, you can go and see Santa. Wait right here and he will call you. Where are you from? Oh, you're from (name of city or town.) I'm so glad you came to see us!"

She knows how to talk to children and put them at ease. However, the Snow Queen can't talk too much to her young visitors and lose track of what she needs to do for Santa. While she provides gentle encouragement to the very shy youngsters,

Lisa Ramos is the object of affection of an adoring little fan.

47

Snow Queen Lisa Ramos coaxes a shy visitor. Photo courtesy of Lisa Ramos.

she occasionally has to hold back the overly-eager ones who want to rush past her straight to Santa's lap. Then there are some little visitors who are all too happy just to stay with the Snow Queen.

Santa laughed, "Sometimes I look over and see little girls who don't want to leave the beautiful Snow Queen. They want to have their pictures taken with her and many will even try to dress like her."

Indeed, the Snow Queen has inspired many young girls to follow in her footsteps.

Christine Garten said things "clicked" for her about Snow Queen when she was five years old. "She was so sweet, beautiful, kind and sparkly," Christine recalled. "I loved the dress, the twinkly shoes, her tiara!"

For her, being Snow Queen was a dream come true. At the age of eighteen, she was chosen by Downtown Presents to have the role at the Sixth Street Marketplace.

"The costume makes you feel so pretty, you can't help but sparkle," she said. "It makes me feel special, then I can make the children feel special and see the sparkle in their eyes."

"It is such an honor to be Snow Queen," Christine said. "I feel so blessed because I love these children so much. Each one brings a piece of magic to us. You see the awe in their little faces. I truly feel that I receive so much more than I give."

Christine affirmed the importance of each child's moment onstage. "It's just you and that person," she said. "It's not like a conveyor belt. And it doesn't matter about their socio-economic level, their clothes or anything else. All of them are special for that moment and we love each one."

Snow Queen Alison Duncan with one of Santa's youngest visitors. Photo courtesy of Alison Duncan.

LEGENDARY SANTA'S STORIES FROM THE CHAIR

"For me, being Snow Queen is more than wearing the dress or tiara," Christine said. "You unfold into this role. You grow into it."

She tells her own daughter, Darden. "Beauty comes from the inside." She has been taking Darden to see Legendary Santa since she was two months old.

Legendary Santa agreed. "Each Snow Queen needs to have great interior beauty - kindness, love of children, goodness, patience, and an ability to engage children and their parents as they get ready to visit Santa. She should be young and confident and always ready to go the extra mile for a child," he said.

❄

Kristin Hardwick knew she wanted to be a Snow Queen "as soon as I could walk!" She first saw Legendary Santa at the age of six months. She had to wait until she was sixteen to be considered for the role of Snow Queen. She was Snow Queen while Legendary Santa was located in the Richmond Convention Center.

"Snow Queen starts the magic," Kristin said. "Children grow up so fast. It's nice to see 12-year-olds who still believe in Santa. It keeps them young."

Sometimes she has used the magical "Snowflake of Courage" to soothe nervous youngsters before their big moment with Santa.

"There was one little girl who was so scared," Kristin recalled. "I reached up and gave her a snowflake from the Christmas tree. After that, she went ahead and sat in Santa's lap."

Kristin, who teaches children with special needs, remembered one young man who came to see Santa. "This young man has some struggles," she said.

Kristin Hardwick as Snow Queen in 2005. Photo courtesy of Kristin Hardwick.

Kristin Hardwick as a baby in 1988. Photo courtesy of Kristin Hardwick.

49

LEGENDARY SANTA'S STORIES FROM THE CHAIR

"But Santa would take extra time with him. He really cares about each and every child. People can feel that, you know."

There have been some humorous moments as well for the Snow Queens, both inside and outside of Santa Land. Often babies will reach up and pull off the Snow Queen's tiara or youngsters will hug a little too hard. But when a child recognizes the Snow Queen out in public, the moment can be awkward.

"I try to stay in character," said Kristin, who was spotted by a young girl when she was leaving the theatre after a show. "The little girl stopped and shouted 'That's Snow Queen!'" Kristin laughed. She didn't want to spoil the magic since she was not in costume, "So I just said hello and kept going!"

The Snow Queen knows that many little girls dream of sitting in her chair one day.

Alicia Talley beams as Snow Queen 2010.

This Snow Queen has a very young admirer.

50

Alison Duncan has also relied on the "Snowflake of Courage." "When I give them this gift, many do not experience fear anymore. I also tell them how nice Santa is and that he is one of my best friends."

Alison has been a Snow Queen since 1998, starting out in Sixth Street Marketplace, then moving to the Richmond Convention center and finally to the Children's Museum of Richmond. Like other Snow Queens, she had visited Legendary Santa every year since she was a baby.

She brings her own vivid memories of visiting Santa as a child to her Snow Queen persona. "Getting dressed up to go to the Tea Room at Miller and Rhoads, listening to Eddie Weaver play the organ, visiting the Fawn shop to purchase gifts for my parents, and talking to Bruce the Spruce and Snow Bear. These memories will stay with me much longer than an average trip to the local mall Santa," Alison noted.

Alison enjoys seeing the older children and young adults visit Legendary Santa. "It is a sign that the experience does not stop even if they have grown up," she said.

"When you visit Legendary Santa, you encounter an experience that is so much more than just telling him what you want for Christmas," Alison said. "Visiting Santa Land thrusts you into a spellbinding atmosphere full of wonderment."

She laughs about the families with numerous members all trying to squeeze into the picture with Santa. "To me, that is the true meaning of tradition and legacy," said Alison. "With Legendary Santa, this kind of picture happens at least a few times a day!"

She is deeply touched by children with special needs who come to see their beloved Santa.

"These children, who may be autistic, have Down Syndrome, cerebral palsy, etc. have so much joy in their hearts and so much spirit about visiting with us. Even if they can't speak, you see the adoration in their facial expressions that they are truly happy to be there," Alison said.

LEGENDARY SANTA'S STORIES FROM THE CHAIR

Jessica Dodson understands what it takes to be a good Snow Queen as well. "You must be kind, outgoing, and friendly. You must also be able to endure many scared children. Some little ones cry a lot before going to see Santa. This takes some practice to be able to stay with Santa for eight hours with busy lines at the Children's Museum."

Jessica, who wanted to be "part of the magic," brings a natural love of working with children to her role. "My favorite thing is to dress up and play with the little ones."

※

As Snow Queen, she tries to help children calm down their jitters when they come up to the stage. "I like to compliment every little boy and girl, because I feel like a couple of kind words go a long way. I also give kids a chance to practice their list. Some little girls really look up to me because I am a Queen, much like the Disney Princesses," she said.

The Snow Queens are the first to hear some of the special requests that the children will make of Santa. Often, they ask for something besides toys, which can make for emotional moments.

Jessica remembers three incidents.

"I asked a young lady what she was going to ask for and she replied 'A new heart for my mom, the one she has now isn't good, and I think she needs a new one.'"

"Another little girl said that she wanted her grandma to get better and to have a good Christmas. I asked if there was anything else she wanted, and she said there are some things that she might like, but all she really wants is for her grandma to have a good Christmas."

Jessica spoke of a child's letter, which said, " I love you Snow Queen and Santa too, and my sister and God. Please make sure to go to all the orphanages and pounds."

"I thought this was very sweet that they thought of others when it was their big moment to ask for whatever they wanted," she said.

Jess Dodson knows that Santa relies a great deal on his Snow Queen.

※

Lisa Ramos, like most of the Snow Queens, visited Santa at Miller & Rhoads when she was a child. She applied for the

52

A Snow Queen and her Prince Charming

One night in December 2007, as Santa Land was about to close, the manager asked Snow Queen Christine Marsh to stay a few minutes longer to accommodate a special family who was coming in after hours. The manager also told her that her boyfriend, Jimmy Garten, who was coming to see her, was running late.

She agreed but thought it was odd that all the Children's Museum staff had come in and sat down close to the stage. Then she saw her boyfriend walk up to the platform and stand beside Santa.

"Santa said 'Snow Queen, come here right now!'" Christine recalled. He wanted her to sit on his knee and as she did, her future husband took out a ring and proposed to her in front of everyone in Santa Land.

"He couldn't get down on his knee because of my gown," Christine laughed. "And he's such a logical kind of guy, so this was very out of character for him! I was completely shocked."

Such is the magic of Legendary Santa!

role of Snow Queen, coming from a background of training dolphins and sea lions.

"This was more glamorous," she laughed, recalling all the beautiful Snow Queen gowns in the changing room at Miller & Rhoads. "I remember the children treating me as if I were a china doll, with such awe on their faces. It was a precious moment. I also loved the look on the faces of the older kids when Santa called out their names. You could see that they still believed."

Lisa remembers children who gave her flowers; shy children who were not too sure that walking over to Santa was such a good idea; and kids who were so excited they could barely contain themselves.

"Nothing compares to the magical feeling of that time," she said.

LEGENDARY SANTA'S STORIES FROM THE CHAIR

The Snow Queens all noted that the children are not the only ones who get excited about seeing Santa. One day, a mother with four children came into the Thalhimers location and was reminiscing that she had sat on Santa's knee when she was little. The Snow Queen found out about it and told Santa, who called the mother over. She burst into tears and went over to sit on his knee.

Sometimes in Santa Land, improvisation is key. On one memorable occasion, the Snow Queen was running late due to traffic problems. Legendary Santa was ready to go onstage, but could not start without his Snow Queen. The desperate Santa Land photographer spied a young blonde mother in the audience and asked her if she would substitute for Snow Queen. To his amazement, she agreed. She was able to slip into one of the Snow Queen dresses and onto the stage she walked. However her son, who was in the audience with a relative, recognized her and shouted "That's my Mommy!" It took quite a bit of coaxing to get him to calm down. Thankfully, the real Snow Queen soon arrived and took her rightful place onstage with Santa.

While most of the children's visits with Snow Queen and Santa have been very joyful, a few have been difficult for everyone in Santa Land.

Legendary Santa shared one of his most moving stories. "Two years ago, a very ill baby came to visit Santa," he said. "Snow Queen went out of her way when there was a camera problem, to keep Mom and Dad and baby happy. She held the child, who was two or three months old and connected to tubes, wires and swathed in bandages, and took pictures with him. She even took pictures of the parents with the child in front of our Christmas tree while they waited for the camera problem to be fixed."

There was not a dry eye in Santa Land that night.

"There is so much love in that room," Christine Garten said. "We couldn't be who we are without the entire staff – the greeters, the photographer, all the behind-the-scenes people – who make sure things go smoothly. The magic in Santa Land comes from everyone and it enables us to meet the loving needs of each child and child at heart."

LEGENDARY SANTA'S STORIES FROM THE CHAIR

Santa watches as a child presents his list to the Snow Queen, Alicia Talley.

The Snow Queen Scholarship

The Snow Queen made such an impression on Cindy Harrison that she endowed the Snow Queen Scholarship program at the Children's Museum of Richmond.

"I was bedazzled!" she said, recalling her visits to Miller & Rhoads at Christmas in the 1960s with her mother and older sisters. "The Snow Queen had this glow, this magic. She was patient, graceful and would greet each child joyfully."

"Going downtown to Miller & Rhoads was like going to New York City," Cindy said. "It was a big to-do. We'd see the store windows all decorated and we'd buy our Christmas outfits."

Cindy was a diehard follower, later taking her own daughter to see Legendary Santa and Snow Queen as they moved from one site to the next after Miller & Rhoads closed down.

"I remember all those wonderful, graceful, poised, intelligent girls. Snow Queen is something that all young girls can aspire to," Cindy noted. "It's not just about outward beauty. It's about inner beauty."

Realizing what an inspiration the Snow Queen has been to generations of young girls in Richmond, the Children's Museum decided in 2009 to expand the role beyond the holidays by instituting an annual Snow Queen Scholarship. Each year, the scholarship would be awarded to an area high school girl who embodies the qualities of creativity, integrity, hard work and service to others, especially children.

In January, 2010, Alicia Talley was named the first Snow Queen Scholarship recipient at the Children's Museum's annual Snow Days Festival. As the new tradition grows, reigning Snow Queens will crown incoming Queens in this magical and heart-warming ceremony that makes an indelible impression on the next generation of young women. The honor includes making Snow Queen visits and appearances throughout the year and serving as a role model to inspire little girls to reach for their dreams.

Legend of the Snow Queen

In the land of Winter, where nothing was green, there was a kingdom of ice ruled by the Snow Queen. On her blizzard of hair she wore an icicle crown, and the lightest of frosts formed the lace of her gown. Her eyes dazzled like sun-sparkled snow, and the chill in the air gave her cheeks a rose glow. From her castle she'd watch the flurries swirl by, following each flake as it danced through the sky. No matter how long she watched, or how quickly they came, she never saw two that were exactly the same. And though each was different, they made quite a sight, when together, they'd blanket her palace in white.

How delightful! said the Queen with a bright little smile, each snowflake's unique just like every child! And when they all come together in one spot to play, they add laughter and magic to a wintery day.

So, inspired by the wonder of that blanket of snow, the Queen sleighed from her castle to the valley below. She headed to Richmond, where the weather is warm, to bring children the joys of a daily snow storm.

So put on your mittens and come join the play! When the Snow Queen's at CMoR, every day's a Snow Day!

Snow Queen Tiffany Welch, in her element.

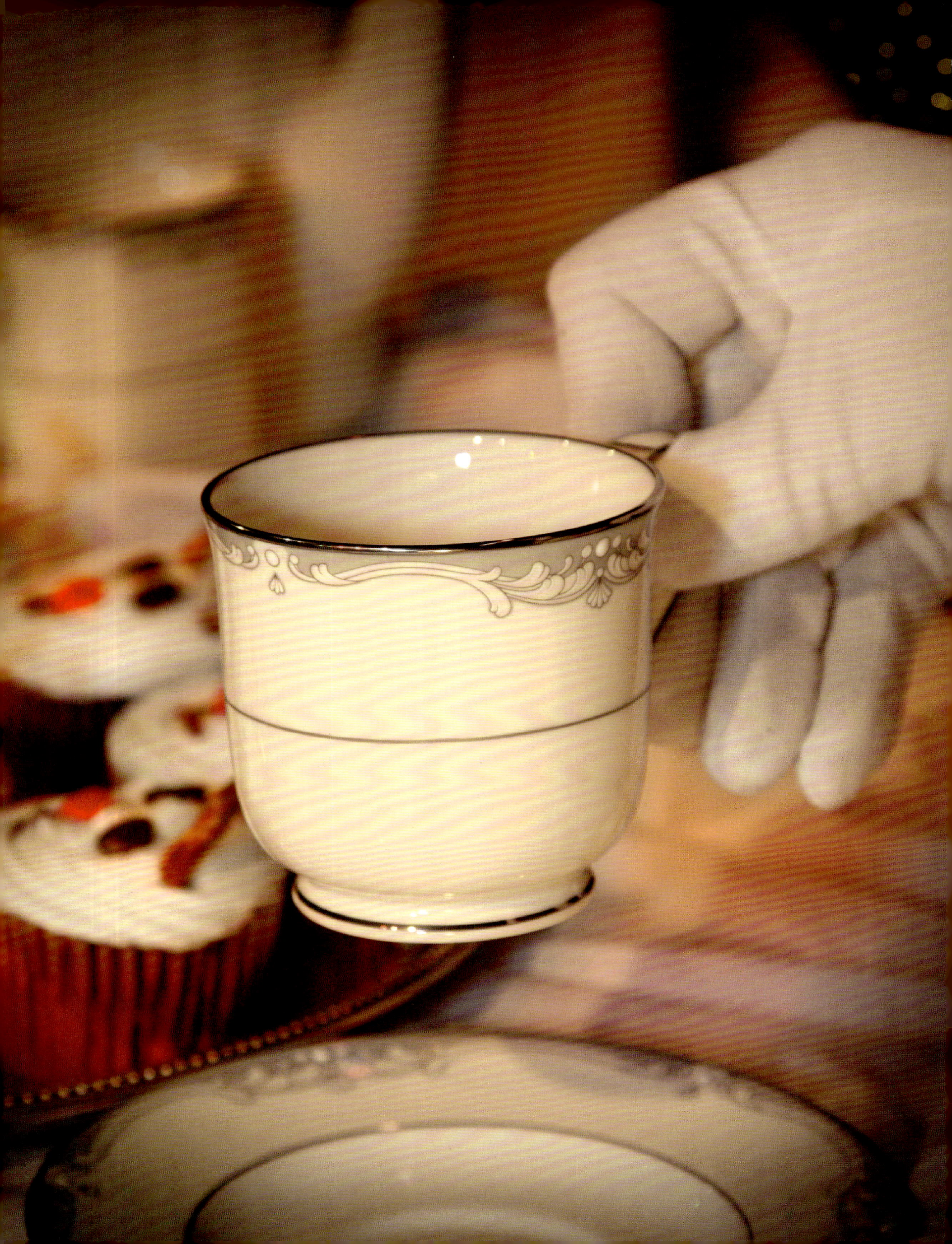

LEGENDARY SANTA'S STORIES FROM THE CHAIR

Tea With Santa… Coming Full Circle

LOCATION: THE HILTON GARDEN INN, 501 E. BROAD ST., DECEMBER 2010

The magical jangle of sleigh bells interrupts the pianist's lively rendition of "We Wish You A Merry Christmas." The boys and girls and moms and dads sitting at the festive tables stop clapping and singing. A current of anticipation courses through the room. The pianist immediately begins playing the jolly melody of "Here Comes Santa Claus."

And just as he had done decades ago, Legendary Santa walked back into Miller & Rhoads to once again host Tea with Santa. His first home in Richmond is now the site of the new Hilton Garden Inn. The owners of the carefully restored building, in cooperation with the Children's Museum of Richmond, have revived the time-honored tradition of the Santa Tea back where it originated. Once again, the grand old landmark resonates with the sounds of Christmas music and children laughing.

Legendary Santa makes his way around to every table in the room, greeting the children, their parents and even their grandparents. The white tablecloths with red and green napkins complement the guests' dressy holiday outfits. Giant nutcrackers stand on display and Christmas trees twinkle with tiny lights. Families enjoy the refreshments as they wait excitedly for Santa to stop at their table.

As Santa makes his merry rounds, Debo Dabney, the pianist, continues to play "Here Comes Santa Claus."

"Sometimes my fingers get so tired because it can take Santa twenty minutes to get around the room and see everybody!" Debo admitted with a laugh.

The Santa Tea comes full circle when Santa greets guests at the Hilton Garden Inn in the former Miller & Rhoads building in 2010. Photo courtesy of the Richmond Times Dispatch.

LEGENDARY SANTA'S STORIES FROM THE CHAIR

Debo Dabney plays the piano at story time at the Santa Tea at the Hilton Garden Inn, 2010. Photo courtesy of John Cario.

Debo knows all the holiday songs well, having played keyboard or piano at the Santa events for twenty years. He started at Sixth Street Marketplace, doing much the same routine that the beloved Eddie Weaver performed with Santa at the Miller & Rhoads Tea Room. Before the sleigh bells announced Santa's pending arrival, Debo was entertaining the audience with Jingle Bells, Frosty the Snowman, the Charlie Brown song and crowd favorites such as the Addams Family theme and the Peter Gunn theme.

At last, Santa has visited with everyone and goes to the stage.

"Are you excited? Have you been good?" he asks all the boys and girls as Debo "ad libs" with musical flourishes on the piano. Santa says the reindeer are excited too. "Dasher, Dancer, Prancer, Vixen, Comet, Cupid, Donner and Blitzen… and of course Rudolph! We're all ready to fly to your house on Christmas Eve!"

Then Santa takes off his white gloves and gets ready to drink his milk to Debo's musical accompaniment. He declares how much he loves milk and downs the glass in one big long gulp.

Kent and Barr Brooks, all dressed up to see Santa in the Tea Room, circa 1948. Photo courtesy of Leigh Davis Rooke.

(Santa has confided that although he loves milk, he much prefers it cold, not room temperature!)

Next Santa brings out the beautiful Snow Queen and escorts her to her chair. Santa asks, "Who's missing?" Debo begins to play the Hi-Ho song from Snow White and the Seven Dwarfs.

"It's the Elf!" Santa says. "Come out, come out wherever you are!" From behind the curtain, the Elf says she is too shy. Finally Santa coaxes her out amidst the cheers of the youngsters.

Santa made a big show of drinking his milk all in one gulp in the original Tea Room.

The energy level in the room rises even more as the Elf runs around the room singing Jingle Bells and handing the microphone to children, urging them to join her. Little girls in red and green plaid dresses whirl and twirl to the music as little boys in coats and ties jump up and down.

"I'm the comedic support," laughs Heather Price, who has been an Elf for several years. "I'm very kid-like. I can get on their level and relate to the children." It doesn't hurt that she comes with a background in children's theatre.

"I can be kind of a liaison too," she added. "Some kids will run straight up to Santa. I can help calm things down. I also answer their questions and I talk to parents and grandparents."

When Debo breaks into "Rudolph, The Red-Nosed Reindeer," everyone knows what is coming.

At the end of the song, the Elf unveils the long-awaited Reindeer Cakes. Years ago, they were served as a sheet cake. Today they are red velvet cupcakes. Santa serves the cupcakes to each eager child. The confections are frosted with white icing and decorated with little pretzel sticks for antlers, chocolate chip eyes and a cinnamon candy nose.

The time-honored routine now has a new component. After serving the Reindeer Cakes, Santa settles into a chair. He reads "The Christmas Mouse" story to the enthralled children sitting on the floor. Snow Queen, at his side, turns the pages.

Then the ever-energetic Elf gets everyone on their feet for one more dance...the Reindeer Boogie. Debo plays the "Hokey-Pokey" song for the melody as youngsters and even parents do the moves to "put your right hoof in, take your right hoof out...."

At last, the party draws to a close.

"I need to go back to the North Pole," Santa says. "So be good and remember that Old Santa loves you!"

The Snow Queen hands out "Tea with Santa" ornaments at the door to the children as they leave. Debo plays "We Wish You A Merry Christmas," as Legendary Santa goes back up the chimney and the sound of sleigh bells fades away.

Debo, whose music flavors the program as much as the Reindeer Cake said, "This brings people from all over. I've watched many of them grow up and bring their kids. It's an all-American tradition."

Honoring that tradition was very important to John Cario, general manager of the Hilton Garden Inn.

"We treasure the history of this building and the memories so many people fondly hold of Christmas at Miller & Rhoads," he said. "We want to bring many of those memories back to life to make our lobby a hub of holiday activity in downtown Richmond." Cario, who grew up in New York City with the tradition of the Macy's Santa, brought a special affinity for the project.

Decorated in the spirit of the store's heyday, the Miller & Rhoads windows once again beckoned onlookers with cheerful displays of train sets, kids with sleds, Sara Sue hats and a Santa scene. At night, the brightly-lit windows created an inviting streetscape adding to the festive sparkle of Richmond's grand illumination. As the windows evoked a nostalgic remembrance of that bygone era, they also offered a glimpse of a promising future for a revitalized downtown district.

For many who attended the Santa Teas in 2010, the Hilton and the Children's Museum succeeded in recapturing the excitement.

Pam Roberts, continuing her long-time tradition of visiting Santa on December 18, went to the Santa Tea. She had come to see Santa at Miller & Rhoads as a child.

Reindeer Cakes, 2010.

Legendary Santa serves his famous Reindeer Cake, circa 1974.
Photo courtesy of Richmond Times-Dispatch.

Pam Roberts came to see Santa with four generations of her family. Photo courtesy of Pam Roberts.

"It brought back such wonderful memories! My daughters kept making fun of me because I was getting so emotional thinking back on the wonderful times we had spent on those trips to see Santa and how quickly the time had passed," she said.

She noted that her mother first brought her sister and her to see the "REAL" Santa in Richmond at Miller & Rhoads in the 1950s. "I continued the tradition with my two daughters, except we always came on December 18, my oldest daughter's birthday. We made the first visit on her first birthday in 1984 and always had lunch in the Tea Room with Santa."

"Those days were such magical memories and being back at the old Miller & Rhoads and seeing the memorabilia and listening to Santa say the same things at the Tea was just too much for this mama! What a great and precious memory we are making through four generations!"

The Tea with Santa actually began as Lunch with Santa in the Miller & Rhoads Tea Room, around the 1950s. The experience of eating a meal with Santa in one of "the South's finest tea rooms" became a delicious and indelible memory for countless visitors. Boys and girls would eat their "Flying Saucer" hamburger or "Snoopy Special" hot dog on linen-covered tables set with china and silver. The mothers, in white gloves and Sara Sue hats, would make certain their children remained on their best behavior. Eddie Weaver, a pillar of the Tea Room's appeal, played Christmas songs on the piano until Legendary Santa and Snow Queen made their grand entrance.

For many Richmonders and those who came to Richmond, visiting the Miller & Rhoads Santa meant much more than simply giving him your Christmas list. Parents and children could spend the better part of a day in Santa Land on the seventh floor, the Tea Room on the fifth floor and the Fawn Shop on the third floor. That doesn't even count the time spent gazing at the spectacular store windows.

Lynn Mitchell of Augusta County paints a vivid picture of them. "At Christmas, those stores seemed magical as they transformed into winter

Eddie Weaver played the piano at the Miller & Rhoads Tea Room. Photo courtesy of the Richmond Times-Dispatch

wonderlands with holiday decorations ... destinations for thousands of Virginia residents to visit ... children standing outside on the sidewalk peering through the plate glass windows watching wide-eyed as animated displays moved and twirled, and visiting inside for shopping, dining, and a stop to see Santa," she wrote in her blog.

"With crowds of other people, we stood on the sidewalk and watched awe-struck as the moving soldiers, busy bears, trains, dolls, forest creatures, and elves moved and twirled in workshops or snowy winter white landscapes ... each window with a different theme. Miller & Rhoads and Thalhimers would compete with one another for the most entertaining and elegant windows ... and the public was the richer for it."

Curry Nelms of Westover Hills in Richmond also loved the windows and Santa's "milk trick."

"Going to Miller & Rhoads to see Santa was a special occasion in my family for many reasons," she said. "One was just the magic of Santa and the whole Christmas season. Walking past the decorated windows on Grace Street started that little excited feeling that you have only as a true believer. Because we were not accustomed to eating dinner in restaurants, part of the magic was going to the Tea Room and having dinner with Santa. Watching Santa eat, I could barely swallow my food and then when he drank an entire glass of milk in one gulp and told us not to try that at home, I was a true believer. Besides, I had tried that at home and it was impossible to drink an entire glass of milk in one gulp!"

Andrew and Stephen Ball enjoy the treats in the Tea Room during Lunch with Santa. Photo courtesy of Sandra Jett Ball.

While the milk made an impression on Curry Nelms, the taste of the Reindeer Cake has stayed with Mythika von Griffyn for many years.

"It had a very special taste," she said. "It was a flat white sheet cake, the icing not too thick. Each slice had its own character, with a snowman or Rudolph design in red and green crystals.

Santa would cut a slice and hand it to you. I remember the crunch of those crystals seemed like magic to me."

Legendary Santa noted, "As I used to tell the kids in the Tea Room, Rudolph made the cake himself and mixed the batter with his hooves. I guess he got a special waiver from the Health Department!"

After visiting with Santa and doing some Christmas shopping, Heather Buffkin of Mechanicsville experienced a very exciting moment in the Tea Room when she was a little girl. She had eaten her favorite lunch of a Jack and Jill peanut butter and jelly sandwich and chocolate milk. Her parents had the Missouri Club. Then they waited for Santa to come to the Tea Room.

"I loved the way that he drank his milk over the microphone and told us not to try this at home. My favorite part was when Santa came down the runway to pass out the Reindeer Cake," Heather said. "As I was going to the table to get my cake, I reached up and touched Santa and looked over at my aunt and said 'TOUCHED HIM!' in a really surprised voice. I couldn't believe I actually got to touch Santa when he was in the presence of hundreds of other people!"

She remembers buying various items in the Fawn Shop over the years. "I bought my Dad a tie, wallet, handkerchiefs, and cologne, and I want to say some kind of tie holder that turned. For my Mom, I bought her a rhinestone bracelet, earrings, perfume, picture frame, etc."

For Jane Plum, the Tea Room was special for many reasons.

Snow Queen Donna Deekens with Santa in the Tea Room, waving to guests, 1988. Photo courtesy of Donna Strother Deekens.

A CHILD'S CHRISTMAS AT
Miller & Rhoads

BLITZEN'S BREAKFAST
Good Anytime -
Savory Sausage and Pancakes,
served with butter and syrup. $2.80

COMET'S COMBO
A classic - Juicy hot dog on a bun with buttery
corn on the cob
and potato salad $2.65

CUPID'S CHOICE
Here's the Beef!
Hamburger on a bun with
potato salad and your own corn on the cob.
       $2.75
With cheese $2.95

PRANCER'S PICNIC
All his favorites -
Boneless chicken tenders served with honey
for dipping and including everyone's
favorite picnic food - potato salad and buttery
corn on the cob. $3.85

SANTA'S BEAR BRUNCH
A busy bear needs good food in his tummy for all his very special
projects. Fill up anytime of day with Santa's Bear favorite snack
- perfect for the bear on the run!
Peanut Butter and sweet jelly sandwich served with creamy fruited
yogurt and your own bunch of grapes. $2.65

All items include choice of milk or soft drink and legendary
Rudolf Cake!

For our guests 12 and under

"My family lived in Essex County and came to Richmond for special shopping trips once or twice a month I think, including the annual trip especially to visit Santa," she said. "The memories of the whole day in Richmond are so special—the excitement in the room in spite of long, long lines, the beauty of the Snow Queen, the tenderness of Santa's voice, the wonder of eating with Santa in the Tea Room in spite of more long, long lines, Eddie Weaver's music, the selection of rolls and muffins in the bun warmer," she said.

Today, the taste of a simple Reindeer Cake evokes delicious memories of a time gone by for Richmonders. It is but one ingredient of a beloved ritual that has emerged from the mists of nostalgia to be new and vibrant again.

"I am very grateful to the Hilton and the Children's Museum for reviving this tradition at the Miller & Rhoads location," said Santa. "It truly feels like we have come full circle."

Autumn Ayres gets ready to enjoy a Reindeer cupcake

Santa's Singing Elf

Desiree Roots didn't know when she went to her first lunch with Santa in the Miller & Rhoads Tea Room, wearing her Christmas dress and white gloves, that one day she would be Santa's Singing Elf. She also didn't know in 1994, after signing on to be the Elf for a year at Sixth Street Marketplace, that she would end up staying for fourteen years!

"I absolutely loved it!" she exclaimed.

Desiree was working for the Richmond Jazz Society at the time and was well-known in local music circles. She had been singing since she was four in the children's choir and first performed professionally at the age of thirteen at Haymarket Dinner Theatre. She also did children's plays with Theatre IV. Her talents quickly established the Singing Elf as an important part of Santa's "entourage" and a crowd favorite.

As the ever-mischievous Elf, she would make Santa think she was coming out of one door, then pop out of another. Sometimes she would sneak around and tap Santa on one shoulder and make him look in the opposite direction of where she was. All her tricks elicited peals of laughter from her pint-sized audience.

"I would ask the kids about what they ate for Thanksgiving – like did anyone have Brussels Sprouts or spinach and they would scream NOOOO!" Desiree laughed. "Then I would say they had to guess the name of a song with me only singing one note. I would start with "Ohhhhhh-hhh….and hold the note as long as I could before someone would guess "Oh, You'd Better Watch out, Santa Claus is coming to town!"

Desiree Roots was a Singing Elf for Santa at Sixth Street Marketplace in 1998. Photo courtesy of Desiree Roots Centeio.

One of her favorite moments involved the Reindeer Cake. Her job was to pull off the tablecloth that covered the cupcakes, after Santa told how the reindeer mixed the batter with their hooves. "The kids would just squeal when I pulled off the cloth," she said. "That never got old!"

During her fourteen years as the Singing Elf, Desiree would have two children of her own. She described how Chris Risatti, the director of Downtown Presents, which managed the Legendary Santa program for a time, altered a costume to make a "maternity elf dress" for her. "One little boy saw me and said 'The Elf is pregnant!' " Desiree chuckled. "I asked him how did he think we had so many little elves?"

"One of the joys of this job has been to see families come back year after year and to watch their children grow up," she said. "One lady brought all the pictures of her kids through the years to show me. They had grown taller than the Elf!"

For anyone who may have doubts about the "realness" of Santa, Desiree has her own proof. She once worked in the office at Downtown Presents and confessed that one day she and her co-workers were all "cutting up" a little bit. Later when she went to work as the Elf, she said that Santa, "with a twinkle in his eye," asked her if she'd been good. She replied that yes, of course she had been good.

"Then Santa looked at me over his glasses and said, "Elf, I mean have you really been good?" Desiree recalled. "Somehow he knew!"

After all, he is Legendary Santa.

Here's a sampling of some of

Jingle Bells

Dashing through the snow
In a one horse open sleigh
O'er the fields we go
Laughing all the way
Bells on bob tails ring
Making spirits bright
What fun it is to laugh and sing
A sleighing song tonight

Oh, jingle bells, jingle bells
Jingle all the way
Oh, what fun it is to ride
In a one horse open sleigh
Jingle bells, jingle bells
Jingle all the way
Oh, what fun it is to ride
In a one horse open sleigh

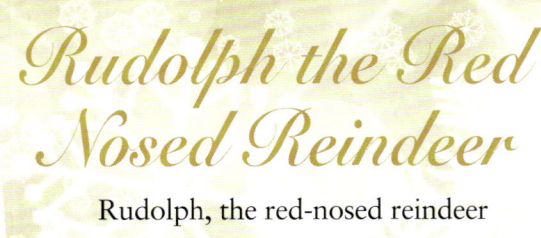

Rudolph the Red Nosed Reindeer

Rudolph, the red-nosed reindeer
had a very shiny nose.
And if you ever saw him,
you would even say it glows.

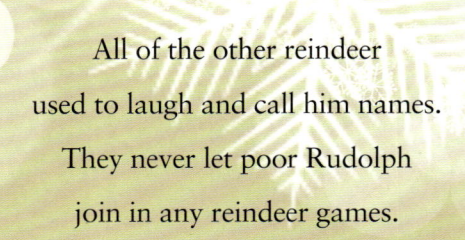

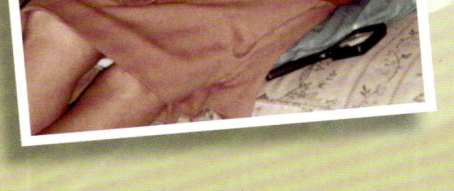

All of the other reindeer
used to laugh and call him names.
They never let poor Rudolph
join in any reindeer games.

70

he songs from Tea with Santa.

Then one foggy Christmas Eve
Santa came to say:
"Rudolph with your nose so bright,
won't you guide my sleigh tonight?"

Then all the reindeer loved him
as they shouted out with glee,
Rudolph the red-nosed reindeer,
you'll go down in history!

Here Comes Santa Claus

Here comes Santa Claus,
Here comes Santa Claus,
Right down Santa Claus Lane,
Vixen and Blitzen and all his reindeer
Pullin' on the reins.
Bells are ringin', children singin',
All is merry and bright.
So hang your stockings and say your prayers,
'Cause Santa Claus comes tonight.

Here comes Santa Claus,
Here comes Santa Claus,
Right down Santa Claus Lane,
He's got a bag that's filled with toys
For boys and girls again.
Hear those sleigh bells jingle jangle,
Oh what a beautiful sight,
So jump in bed, and cover your head,
'Cause Santa Claus comes tonight.

Here comes Santa Claus,
Here comes Santa Claus,
Right down Santa Claus Lane,
He'll come around when chimes ring out,
It's Christmas time again.
Peace on earth will come to all,
If we just follow the light,
So let's give thanks to the Lord above
'Cause Santa Claus comes tonight.

Here comes Santa Claus,
Here comes Santa Claus,
Right down Santa Claus Lane,
Vixen and Blitzen and all his reindeer
Pullin' on the reins.
Bells are ringin', children singin',
All is merry and bright,
So jump in bed, and cover your head,
'Cause Santa Claus comes tonight.

Peace on earth will come to all,
If we just follow the light,
So let's give thanks to the Lord above
'Cause Santa Claus comes tonight,
So let's give thanks to the Lord above
'Cause Santa Claus comes tonight.

Frosty the Snowman

Frosty the Snowman
Was a jolly happy soul
With a corncob pipe and a button nose
And two eyes made out of coal
Frosty the Snowman
Is a fairytale they say
He was made of snow

But the children know
How he came to life one day
There must have been some magic
In that old silk hat they found
For when they placed it on his head
He began to dance around
Frosty the Snowman
Was alive as he could be
And the children say
He could laugh and play
Just the same as you and me
Frosty the Snowman
Knew the sun was hot that day
So he said let's run
And we'll have some fun
Now before I melt away
Down to the village
With a broomstick in his hand
Running here and there
all around the square
Saying catch me if you can
He led them down the streets of town
Right to the traffic cop
And he only paused a moment when
He heard him holler stop
Frosty the Snowman
Had to hurry on his way
But he waved goodbye
Saying don't you cry
I'll be back again some day
Thumpety thump thump
Thumpety thump thump
Look at Frosty go
Thumpety thump thump
Thumpety thump thump
Over the hills of snow

LEGENDARY SANTA'S STORIES FROM THE CHAIR

We Wish You A Merry Christmas

We wish you a Merry Christmas;
We wish you a Merry Christmas;
We wish you a Merry Christmas and a Happy New Year.
Good tidings we bring to you and your kin;
Good tidings for Christmas and a Happy New Year.

Oh, bring us a figgy pudding;
Oh, bring us a figgy pudding;
Oh, bring us a figgy pudding and a cup of good cheer.
We won't go until we get some;
We won't go until we get some;
We won't go until we get some, so bring some out here.

We wish you a Merry Christmas;
We wish you a Merry Christmas;
We wish you a Merry Christmas and a Happy New Year.

Merry Christmas

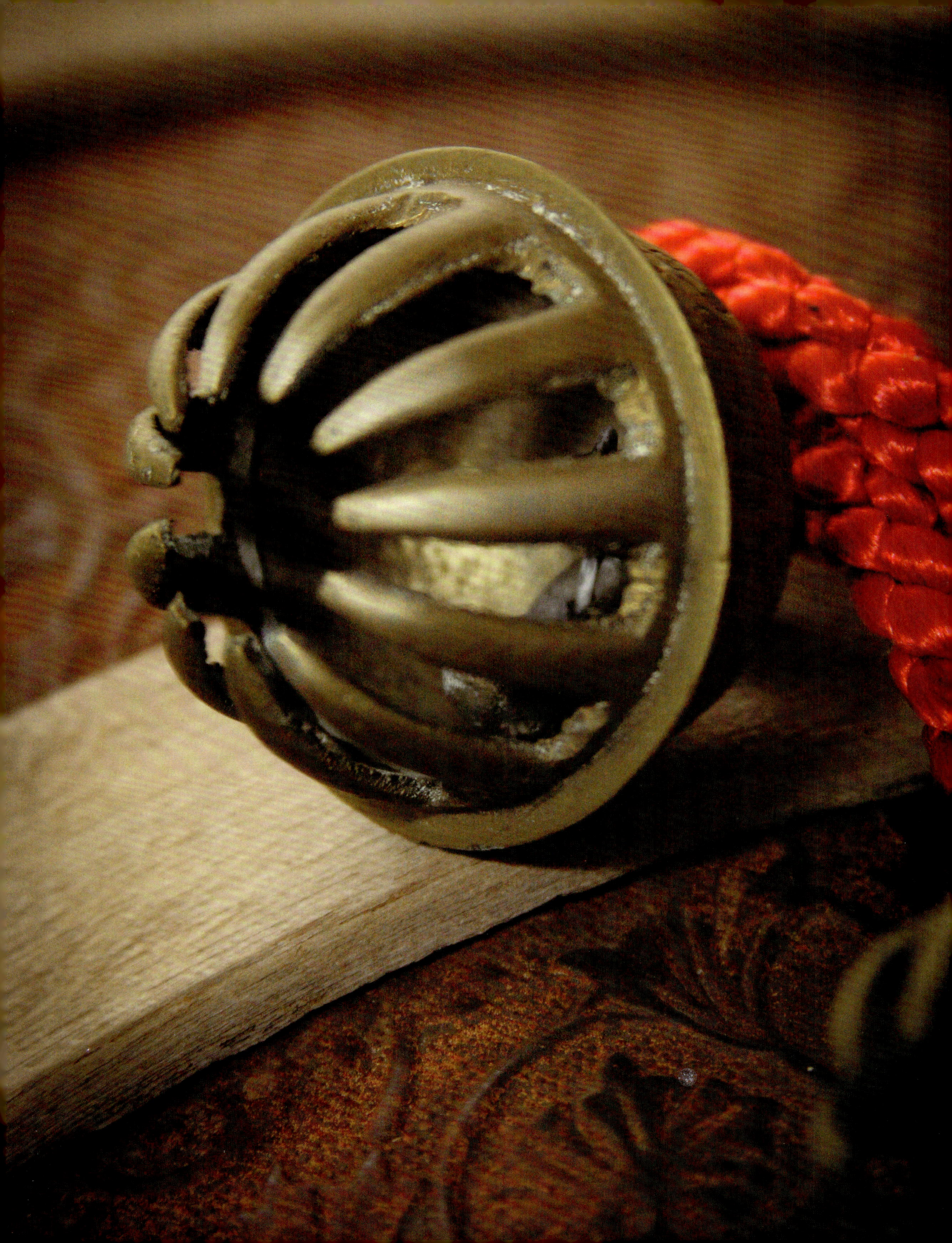

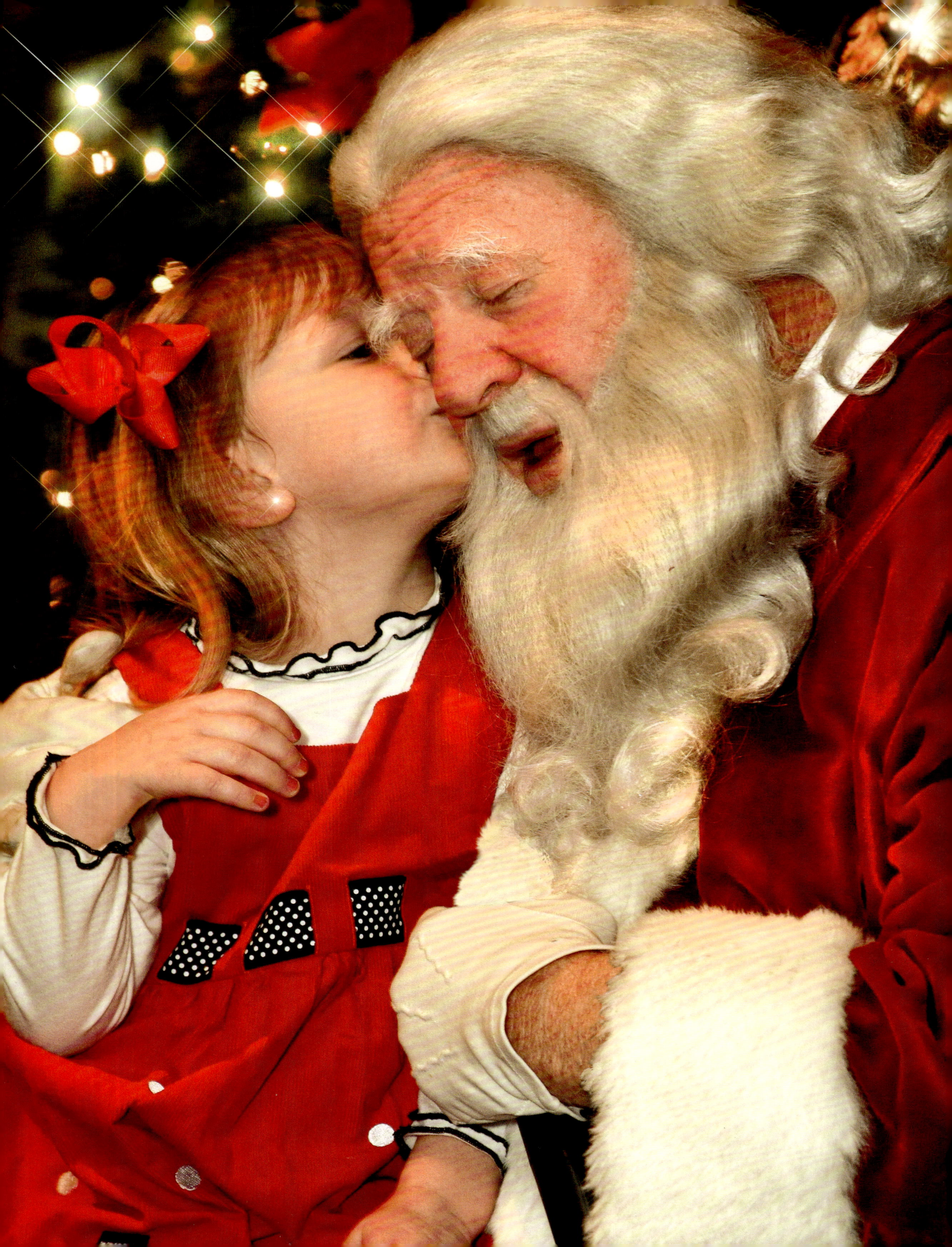

LEGENDARY SANTA'S STORIES FROM THE CHAIR

Santa's Favorite Stories from the Chair

I (This chapter is in Legendary Santa's voice as he recounted some of his favorite stories.)

I have so many wonderful memories from the last seventy-five years in Richmond. Sitting in this chair has given me a great perspective on what people see as the true spirit of Christmas, as well as the lessons we can learn. This chair has also given me so many special memories over the years. I am delighted to share some of my favorite stories, along with my gratitude to all the wonderful people who helped create them.

Maybe the best way to share some of my favorite stories is to start with those about children. And that means starting with the pacifiers! I have bags of them. In fact, I have so many that I keep a "pacifier tree" at my home at the North Pole!

You may wonder why Legendary Santa has bags of baby pacifiers. It's become something of a rite of passage. Parents tell their little ones that Santa will bring them a present if they give up their pacifier or "paci." Sometimes children tell me they want me to give their "pacis" to other babies. Sometimes the Snow Queen and I have worked together to gently persuade a little one to give up this treasured item. We would tell the toddler that I had a special collection of pacifiers and would add his to my pacifier tree that season.

So giving the pacifier to Santa means a child has taken an important step in growing up.

I always take the pacifier and drop it in my boot, since my pants don't have any pockets. That way the child knows I'm keeping their "paci" so I can take it home for my special little tree.

Santa holds some of the many pacifiers that children give him as a rite of passage from their babyhood.

LEGENDARY SANTA'S STORIES FROM THE CHAIR

Children give me other things as well. They know that chocolate cookies are my favorite, so I get lots of those. They give me candy and even throat lozenges so I won't get a sore throat from talking to so many people.

But I'm very moved when youngsters tell me they are leaving their old toys by the fireplace so I can give them to poor children who don't have as many toys.

Sometimes little children are afraid to come up on stage and see old Santa. I'm convinced there's no muscle stronger than a three-year-old not wanting to come sit on my knee! And often, if one child starts to cry, they all start to cry, like a chain reaction. It seems to be contagious!

Over the years, I've gotten pretty good at figuring out which ones will come over. There is actually kind of a cycle to this.

At age one and two, children don't understand and may cry when they see Santa.

At two and a half, they start to get what Santa is about.

LEGENDARY SANTA'S STORIES FROM THE CHAIR

From age three to seven, they believe in the magic of Santa.

By eight or nine, they become more reserved when they greet Santa and start to question things.

When they are teenagers, they clearly don't want to be in Santa Land!

By the time they are college age, the magic starts to return and they want to do this for their family.

When they are young parents, they write notes to Santa for their babies.

Lastly, as grandparents, they bring their family so they can all relive the tradition.

What an honor it is to be present at all these life stages! It's even more special when a child says, "Mommy, that's the same Santa that's in your picture!"

It's crying time again. Sometimes the much anticipated visits with Santa don't go as planned.

LEGENDARY SANTA'S STORIES FROM THE CHAIR

I remember a little girl about two years old who was very shy about seeing me. She took a few little steps then would stop. I was being very careful not to frighten her and was coaxing her very gently. She got closer and closer and finally she sat in my lap! When scenes like this happen and a child runs over to my open arms, often the whole audience gets teary-eyed!

I'm especially proud of another young lady. Her name is Halie Sadler, the daughter of Hermie and Angie Sadler. Halie has autism and, not unlike other young children, she was afraid of coming over to see me. Her sisters would sit on my lap but Halie would walk right past the Christmas tree and me. However, as she grew older, she was able to overcome her fear and sit on my knee and even speak into the microphone. Now she says she loves old Santa!

Cora, Halie and Naomi Sadler come from Emporia to visit Santa just like their parents did as children. Photo courtesy of Angie Sadler.

Of course at the other end of the spectrum are the kids who get a little too excited when they come to see me. I've been nearly choked to death by hugs, hit like a linebacker, had my beard and hair pulled with kids asking if it's real. And yes, sometimes children have "accidents" in my lap. When that happens, old Santa has to go check on the reindeer!

As you know, children dress in their holiday finest when they come to see me. One day a little girl wearing a beautiful white lace dress came and sat on my knee. You could tell the dress was not new, but it was in fine condition. The little girl looked angelic and her mother was beaming too. The mother told me she wanted to show me something. She pulled out a photo and it was her as a little girl in the very same dress. She had saved it all these years so her little girl could wear it to see me. That brought a tear to old Santa's eye!

It's a fashion parade as children dress in their holiday finest to see Legendary Santa.

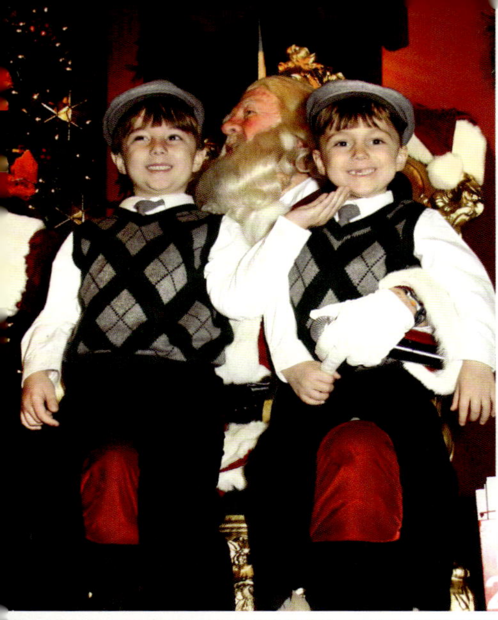
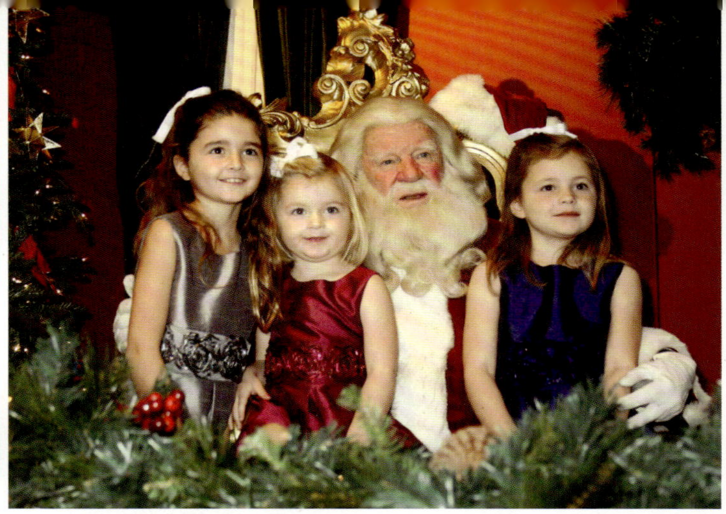
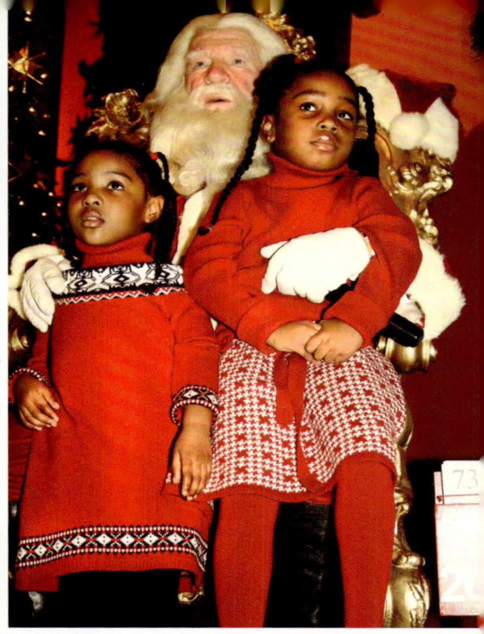
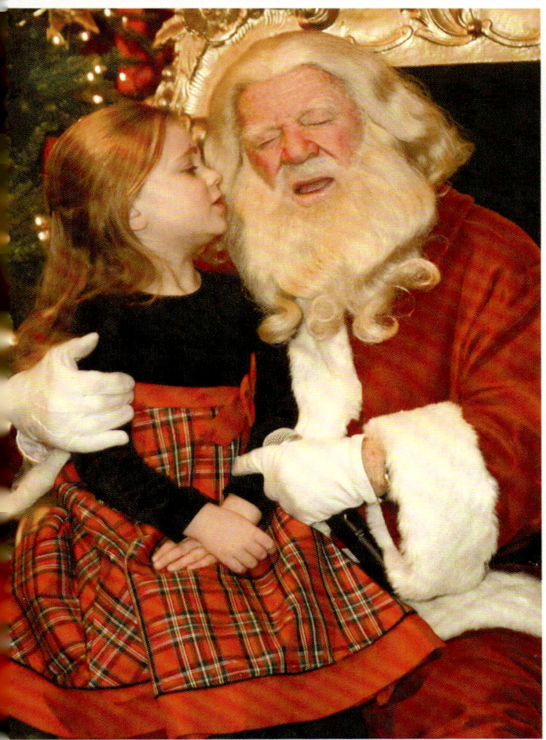
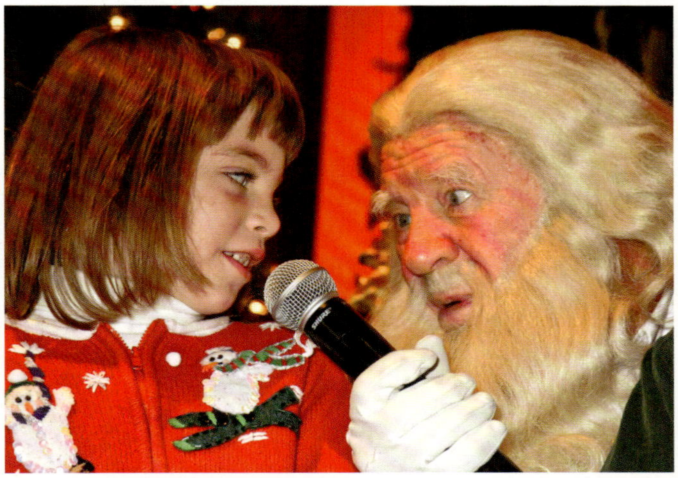
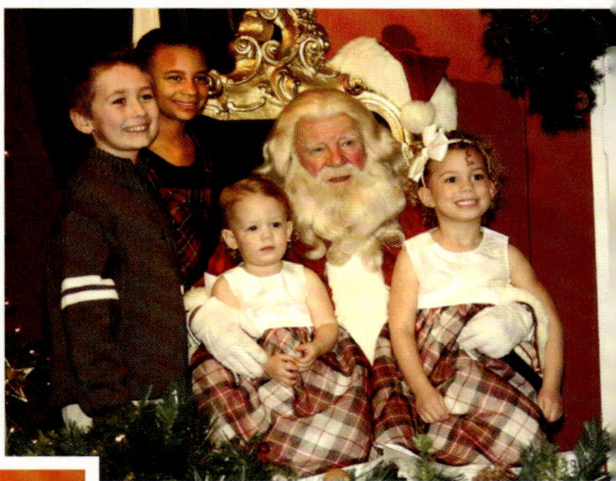
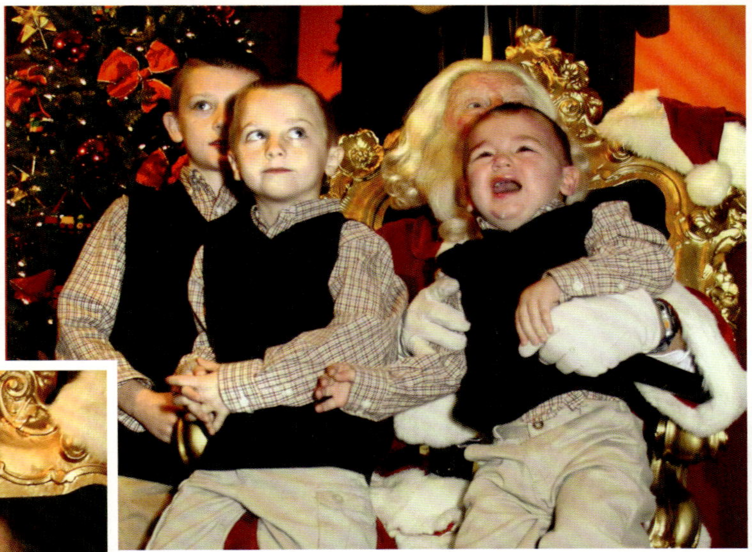
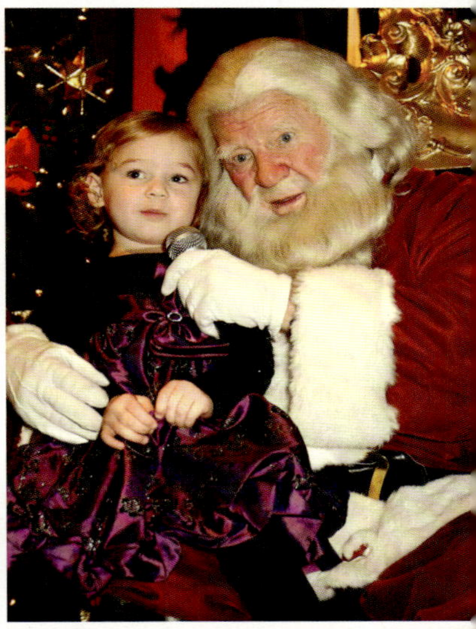
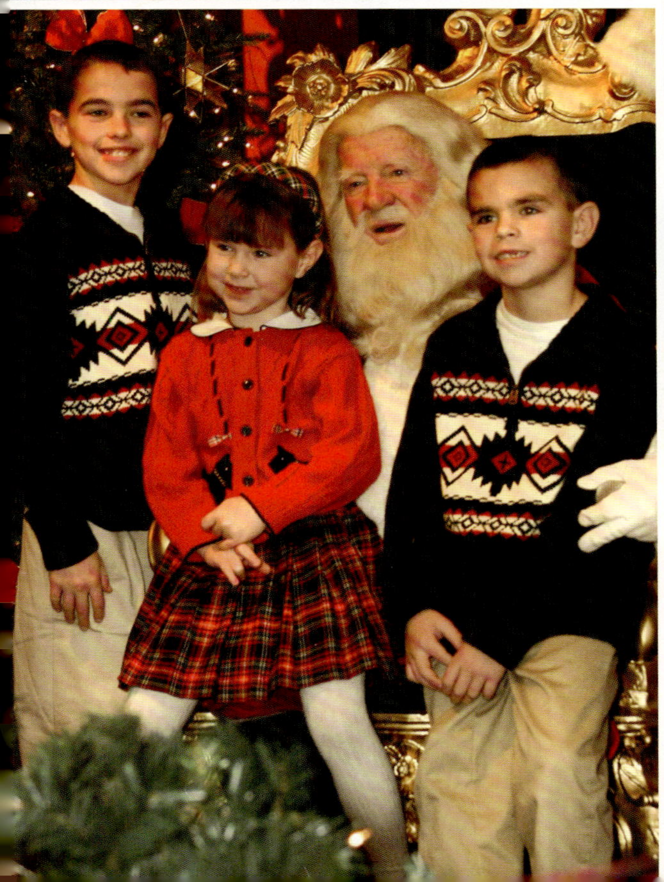
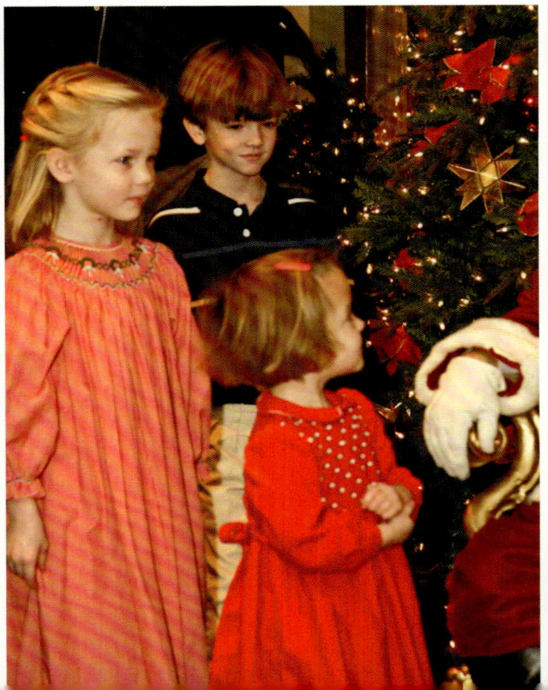
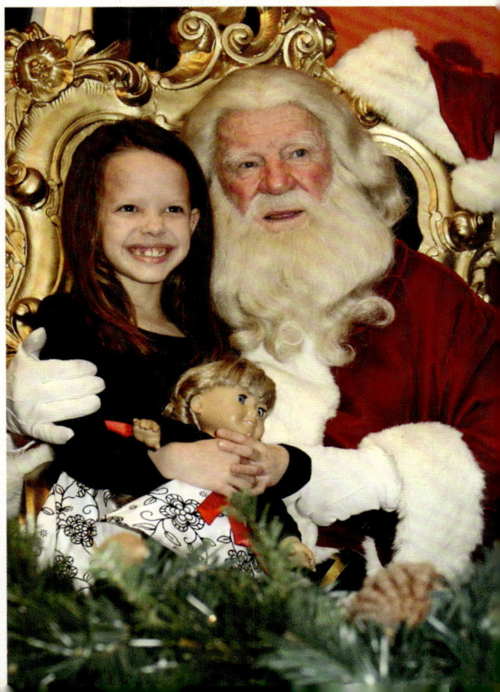

LEGENDARY SANTA'S STORIES FROM THE CHAIR

A visit from Santa has brightened a stay in the hospital for many a child. Photo courtesy of Richmond Times-Dispatch.

While I have many delightful memories of the children who have sat on my knee for the past seventy-five years, there are some situations that were pretty tough for old Santa. The only thing that made them bearable was that I was able to bring a little joy to those in need, even if it was all too brief.

Many years ago, there was a ten-year-old boy who was suffering from terminal kidney disease. Miller & Rhoads sent a limo for him and his parents to treat them to lunch with Santa. The little boy sat at the table with the Snow Queen and me as our guest of honor. Even though he was sickly and pale, he brightened up considerably as he enjoyed his special moment.

At that time there was a character named Felix the Clown who came to Santa Land with Amelia, his pet pig, to entertain all the boys and girls. Their act had little to do with Christmas, but the kids loved it. Felix and Amelia made an appearance and this little boy got to feed Amelia from her baby bottle. I'm told that he talked about that experience until the time he passed away. What a privilege it was to know we helped to bring a little Christmas cheer to him and to his parents during the last days of his life.

One of my most heart-wrenching experiences occurred with a young couple who came in with their twin babies. They had been standing in line with their newborn girls for over two hours to see me. If the Santa Land staff had known their story, they would have brought them over right away.

When this nicely dressed young couple, cradling their beautiful babies dressed in tiny red velvet Christmas frocks, walked over to see me, I could tell that something was amiss. As proud new parents, they should have been beaming with smiles. But there was an air of sadness about them. Then, the tears began welling up as the young mother told me how she and her husband had always come to see Santa when they were kids and couldn't wait to bring their own children when the time came.

Now here they were with their two precious infants and Legendary Santa. The young father began to talk, as the mother became too choked up to continue. He explained that one of the babies was very sick and did not have long to live. This would be their first and only Christmas with both babies. In this brief window of time together as a family, one of the few things the young couple wanted was a photo of their newborn twins with Legendary Santa.

LEGENDARY SANTA'S STORIES FROM THE CHAIR

Old Santa had to really pull himself together for this photo session as the young couple gently placed the baby girls in my arms. They turned their tiny, sweet faces to me, with that liquid gaze of newborns that pours right into your heart. As I gazed down at the babies, the very souls of innocence, I could imagine all the wonderful things their loving parents had planned for them. Birthday parties, learning to ride their first bicycle, starting kindergarten. Wonderful things that one of the twins would come to know, but that the other would never see. And I wished mightily that I had the power to spare this family from the sorrow that was soon to come.

But I knew I did have the power to give them the special moment they needed so much. I tenderly held the babies for their photos as the parents stood next to me. In the photo, I'm sure my cheeks were a little redder and my eyes a little brighter with unshed tears. But we were able to bestow a priceless gift on this little family …a moment in time that would be irreplaceable. For me, it was a moment that will always be unforgettable.

One year, a family came in with their very ill son in a wheelchair. He was about eight or nine years old, too sick to speak. But how he smiled when his father lifted him out of his wheelchair and put him in my lap! The parents were crying as they told me that the boy may not be here next Christmas. It was an enormous responsibility, as well as an enormous privilege, to be entrusted with such a meaningful moment for these parents and their child. They felt that Santa gave them something so special with that photo, but in truth, they gave me much more.

A very special young man has been coming to see me since he was a little boy. He's about thirty now and has autism. His elderly mother brings him each year. He has grown very large and has to use a walker to get around. We let him come in a different way so he does not have to stand in line.

The Elf helps with his walker as my special friend makes his way to my chair. I hear more than a few sniffles in the audience as he slowly moves his great bulk up the ramp to the stage. He's very excited and giggling as I call him by name and say "Come on over to see old Santa!" The children in the audience instinctively know this is a special moment and they do not act impatient. I am proud to see them learning to have compassion for someone who is different, someone who has grown up physically but is still very child-like.

The young man, even at this age and size, still wants to sit on my lap and the Elf helps him. I ask him if he wants Christmas presents and surprises. He giggles and hands me his list. But I don't really

LEGENDARY SANTA'S STORIES FROM THE CHAIR

Arie Brandon of Richmond had a touching experience with Legendary Santa under unusual circumstances.

In 1990, she was a patient in the neurological intensive care unit at the Medical College of Virginia Hospital with a full-blown case of Guillian-Barre Syndrome (a rare autoimmune disease that causes muscle weakness). It had been approximately forty-eight days since she was transferred from Stuart Circle Hospital. Arie would spend a total of fifty-eight days in the ICU.

A young man whose name was Steve occupied the unit adjacent to hers. He was sixteen years old and paralyzed with a broken neck. One day, the ICU was all abuzz with the news that Santa was coming to visit Steve. The nurses were excited and talking about it all day long.

Legendary Santa not only visited the young man, he also stopped by to see Arie.

"When Santa walked into my unit, I was so surprised that he would take the time to visit a 54-year-old woman!" Arie exclaimed. "He wished me a Merry Christmas and said he hoped I got better!" She added that many people are not aware of Santa's many volunteer hours, as he had come to the hospital after putting in a full day at Santa Land.

In 1991, Arie's husband took her downtown to visit Legendary Santa. At that time she was still recovering and walking with the aid of a cane. Santa was not there, but after explaining to the attendants the purpose of her visit, they gave her a special telephone number.

Several days later she called Santa to thank him for visiting her at MCV. She explained who she was and inquired about Steve. She found out that Steve had learned to paint by holding a brush in his teeth. He was paralyzed from the neck down.

This memory is still fresh in her mind. "I can tell that Santa is a very caring person," she said. "After all, how many people get a hospital visit from Legendary Santa?"

need it. We share a very unique form of communication developed over the years, one that is unspoken and yet deeply understood.

I tell him "Be good for old Santa. I can't wait to see you next year!" He nods and gives me a big hug. The Elf helps him get his walker and he pushes his walker back over to his mother, who has been standing offstage. She says, "You did such a good job!" as she and her son walk over to get their pictures. And he did do a good job…a good job of showing that Christmas is for all children.

I had a "Miracle on 34th Street" moment a few years ago. You may remember in the movie where the little Dutch girl went with her adoptive mother to see Santa at Macy's in New York City. The little girl did not speak English, so Santa started speaking with her in her native tongue. Her face lit up and with great mutual enjoyment, she and Santa sang a little song about "Sinter Klaas," which is Dutch (and German) for Saint Nicholas.

In almost the same circumstances, a little German boy came with his new American family to visit me. His big eyes peered out from under a mop of hair as he took in all the sights of Santa Land. I remember that his clothes were too big for him, as if his new brothers, who were older, had given him some of their clothes.

The little boy did not speak English so you can imagine his surprise when I addressed him by name and said "Guten Tag," which is German for good day. I asked him "Wie gehts?" or "How are you?" He became very excited, bouncing up and down on my knee, when I asked him what he wanted Sinter Klaas to bring him for Christmas. All he wanted was a certain kind of chocolate, probably the kind he had enjoyed in his homeland.

LEGENDARY SANTA'S STORIES FROM THE CHAIR

As we chatted back and forth, the boy's parents were laughing. I assumed it was with delight at the notion that Santa could speak German to their son. Later they told me that I was speaking a different dialect from the boy and some things were getting "lost in translation." Nevertheless, they were enormously grateful that Santa had connected with their son on his own level and made him feel included in their tradition during his first Christmas in a new home.

Coming to see Santa should be a happy occasion. But it's not for some children whose world is in turmoil. I see far too many of them suffering from the effects of the bad economy, crime, the wars in the Middle East. What touches me the most are the little ones who ask me to keep their Mom or Dad safe in Iraq or Afghanistan; to help their parent get a job; to help a sick grandparent get better.

I remember one little girl, about five years old, who came to see me. She wasn't wearing a nice Christmas dress like so many of the little girls I had seen that day. She appeared slightly disheveled with dirty blonde hair in her eyes, raggedy jeans and a little pink coat that was frayed at the seams. She looked for all the world like a sweet little ragamuffin.

Her grandmother, who had brought her, stood to the side in her plain brown coat, clutching her purse with both hands. Tears began pouring down her careworn face when the little girl, whose mother was serving in Iraq, told me what she wanted for Christmas.

"I just want my Mommy to be safe," she said. She had no list of toys or other requests. This was all she wanted. Her grandmother wiped her eyes as she went to pay for the photos. The Snow Queen later told me that the girl's mother has been injured in a roadside bombing, but the grandmother did not know how badly she was hurt. We found out later that the mother was OK and was able to come home. I know that was the best Christmas present her little girl could ever want.

LEGENDARY SANTA'S STORIES FROM THE CHAIR

I feel that all the children of the world are truly Santa's. It's up to me to find a way to communicate with them. That's why I know many languages, even sign language.

One of my happiest memories is about a little deaf girl who came to see me. She was maybe eight or nine, dressed in a red wool coat with a little bonnet. Her hands were tucked in her pockets. Her mother was at her side, signing to her daughter as they walked over to my chair. As her daughter climbed up on my knee, the mother said she would interpret for me.

LEGENDARY SANTA'S STORIES FROM THE CHAIR

I smiled and said "I can talk with her myself." I signed the daughter's name and the question "How are you and what do you want from Santa?" The little girl was astonished. Her hands flew out of her pockets and she began signing excitedly. Her fingers were flying as she told me she wanted an American Girl doll. Because there is no symbol for "American Girl doll" she was signing each letter at lightning speed. Laughing, I interrupted her with the sign for "slow down." I believe she asked for the Julie doll.

At the end of our visit, I signed for her to be good and to know that "Santa loves you." She bounded off the stage to her mother, who was standing there with tears streaming down her face. At the end of the ramp, the little girl turned back to me smiling and signed "I love you Santa!"

Illustration by Herb Wimble

LEGENDARY SANTA'S STORIES FROM THE CHAIR

Children are not the only ones who will ask me to bring them something other than toys. Some of the wish lists that adults give to me are very touching.

One year, there was a single mother who waited in line over two hours to see me. She had worked hard all her life and faced many challenges trying to raise her two boys alone. She told me how she used to bring her sons to the Miller & Rhoads Tea Room to see me. She would coach them to practice their manners, sit up straight and be sure to say "yes sir" and "no sir."

The boys had outgrown wanting to visit Santa several years ago. She said that Christmas had not been the same since.

She said she came to see me at Sixth Street Marketplace because she was looking for Christmas. She sat on my knee, something she had never gotten to do as a child. She gave me her Christmas list, which reflected the very personal wishes of someone who had always done much for others and now wanted some things for herself. One of the things she wanted was someone who would understand and love her.

I said, "I love you." Her eyes teared up and she said that was the first time in many years that someone had told her that.

Celeste Williams visited Legendary Santa at Sixth Street Marketplace, 1997. Photo courtesy Richmond Times-Dispatch.

I received a very moving letter from a lady who had been coming to see me since she was nine months old. She stayed at the Hilton Garden Inn at the old Miller & Rhoads building, where we began having the Santa Teas again. She said, "I can feel the magic in this building and when I walk on the fifth floor (where the Tea Room was) I thought I could hear your bells jingle."

She gave me a Christmas list asking for items which cannot be bought. Rather she hoped I could apply some of my magic to help the things she wanted come to her. These were:

A job so she could keep her house

To complete her classes for her master's degree

To find someone to share her life with so she wouldn't be alone

All I can do is to say that I will do the best I can to help their dream come true. In the case of a new job, or a spouse, I say that I will do my best and they should do their best.

Two years ago a young man (slightly disabled) asked for his high school diploma. I asked when was he to graduate, and he said if he passed his tests, in January. I told him that I would do everything I could to help, and that he was to study extra hard and try his best and then things should turn out well for him. Later he let me know that he did pass those tests!

Sometimes a little encouragement is the best gift you can give someone!

Some requests are easier to fill and sometimes, good-hearted people do Santa's work for him.

I'll never forget the homeless man who used to come see me, wherever I was located. He would bring me a cup of coffee and the Sunday paper. He had circled the pictures of the Christmas gifts he wanted and written the names of the people they were for. A family behind him in line saw this and told my Elf to let them know what this man wanted. However, because the Santa Land staff was so perceptive and compassionate, they had already gone out to buy the gifts the homeless man wanted. One of Santa's helpers delivered the gifts – things like a radio, gloves, a clock - the next morning in the snow to the place where the homeless man and his friends stayed. The man came up, took the presents without a word and shuffled off. And the next Christmas…he was back again to see Santa.

I continue to marvel at the role that people allow Santa to play in their lives. One time, a young couple came over to show me something. They had been comparing their childhood Santa photos. They discovered that they had consecutive numbers and had been standing in line together, as strangers, all those years ago. They were firmly convinced that a little Santa magic had brought them together, first as children, then as adults!

LEGENDARY SANTA'S STORIES FROM THE CHAIR

On another occasion, a mother, her three children and their grandparents came to see me. The mother was getting lots of pictures made, both individually and in groups, to send to her husband who was serving in Afghanistan. In the meantime, her boys, who were about twelve, ten and eight, gave me their Christmas lists. Their lists were very short and at the top of each list was the request to "keep Daddy safe."

As I was going over their lists with the boys, I saw out of the corner of my eye that their mother was on the phone, crying. Immediately I feared that something bad had happened. But out of the blue, her husband had called from Afghanistan. He had no clue that his family was with Santa at that very moment.

She handed the phone to me and I told him, "Captain, this is Legendary Santa. You have a very nice family here. We want you to come home safely and soon." When I asked him what he wanted Santa to bring him, he said he wanted his kids to have a good Christmas.

Old Santa has a special place in his heart for these military families. They have shown me, time and time again, that they serve their country too, not on the front lines, but certainly on the home front. When the children of soldiers ask me to bring their parents home safe, I tell them that I will

LEGENDARY SANTA'S STORIES FROM THE CHAIR

do my very best. I say that Santa loves your daddy or mommy and appreciates their service to our country.

Sometimes the battlefield is closer to home. I will never forget the children from a foster home who came to Santa Land. They all were from pretty rough backgrounds. One was a ten-year-old girl, who seemed very quiet, not showing the usual demeanor of a child about to have her big moment with Santa.

When I asked her what she wanted for Christmas, she said, "I want to be alive next year."

I was stunned. Then one of the adults with the foster home told me that her brother had been killed in front of her in a drive-by shooting. Old Santa was deeply saddened by this. Not only had this little girl lost her brother, she had essentially lost her childhood and the sense of security that every child should feel in their home.

I told her that I loved her and made her a solemn promise that she would be alive next year. And when Christmas rolled around again, she came back to see me. And this time she had a smile.

Illustration by Herb Wimble

I've had some interesting groups in Santa Land. There were five young men in their twenties who wanted to pose a certain way with me. They showed me a photo of themselves when they were kids, posed the exact same way. They were all brothers and were giving the photo to their parents for their fiftieth wedding anniversary.

They told me how their parents used to make them get up early, get all cleaned up, dress in their best Sunday suits, tame their cowlicks and march off all freshly scrubbed to see the real Santa at Miller & Rhoads. They would gripe and whine about it as they got older, and rough-house with each other in the car to vent their frustration at having to do something that was "for babies." Then, suddenly, they matured and realized how special those visits had been for their parents in bonding the boys together as a family. As they arranged themselves for the new photo, they confessed that this was the first time they had done so without punching each other and arguing about where to stand. Needless to say, their parents were thrilled with the picture!

Another time, twelve members of the Henrico Police Department came to see me for a group picture. Every one of them had sat on my knee as a child. I thought that they were all probably strangers to each other as children, yet here they were, banding together as adults to go see Santa Claus. Just think of a dozen police officers, trained to be tough and strong, and they were like little children, laughing and joking and jostling each other as they all tried to fit into the picture.

I was glad that they could put aside the serious aspect of their jobs for a short while to revisit the more carefree time of their childhood Christmas visits with me.

Often I make visits out in the community to try to spread some Christmas cheer. One place I visited was the Virginia Home for Adults. Miller & Rhoads would wrap up gifts for all the residents. Milton Burke, the store's longtime display coordinator, would drive the van and I would deliver the gifts. I would go to every room. I have told people that if they ever think they have problems, they should go out there for an hour. You see patients painting with the paintbrush in their teeth. There were residents who might not communicate much, but whose eyes would open wide when they saw me and they'd say "Santa!"

I once visited the psychiatric ward at MCV and came upon a man I knew sitting in a wheelchair in the hallway. He was kind of slouched over and his face had a vacant look. Then he saw me walking down the hall and out of the blue he said "Santa." The nurse said it was the first time he had spoken in months. These are the things that make you realize what a profound effect Santa Claus has on people.

LEGENDARY SANTA'S STORIES FROM THE CHAIR

Back in the 1970s, I remember visiting a young man who had been a wrestling champion. He became a paraplegic after a terrible car wreck in which he broke his back. He later married his rehab nurse and they had triplets. When I was in Santa Land at Thalhimer's, he and his wife brought those triplets to sit on my lap.

I have visited with the children at the MCV pediatric unit and with the patients in the burn unit. The burn unit was especially difficult. Many of the patients are swathed in bandages or in pressure garments. You know that they have suffered excruciating pain. You wish that you could hug them and take that pain away. But of course, their environment must be kept extremely sterile due to the danger of infection. Yet even though old Santa could not touch the burn patients physically, nor they touch me, we still connected on a very heartfelt level. You know how old Santa loves smiles. Their brave smiles said it all.

The Snow Queen and I visited the Children's Hospital on Brook Road on many occasions. We would go there after putting in a full day at Miller & Rhoads. A store employee would drive us there. The hospital would give us gifts that had been donated for the children, and we would go from room to room handing out the presents to the little patients.

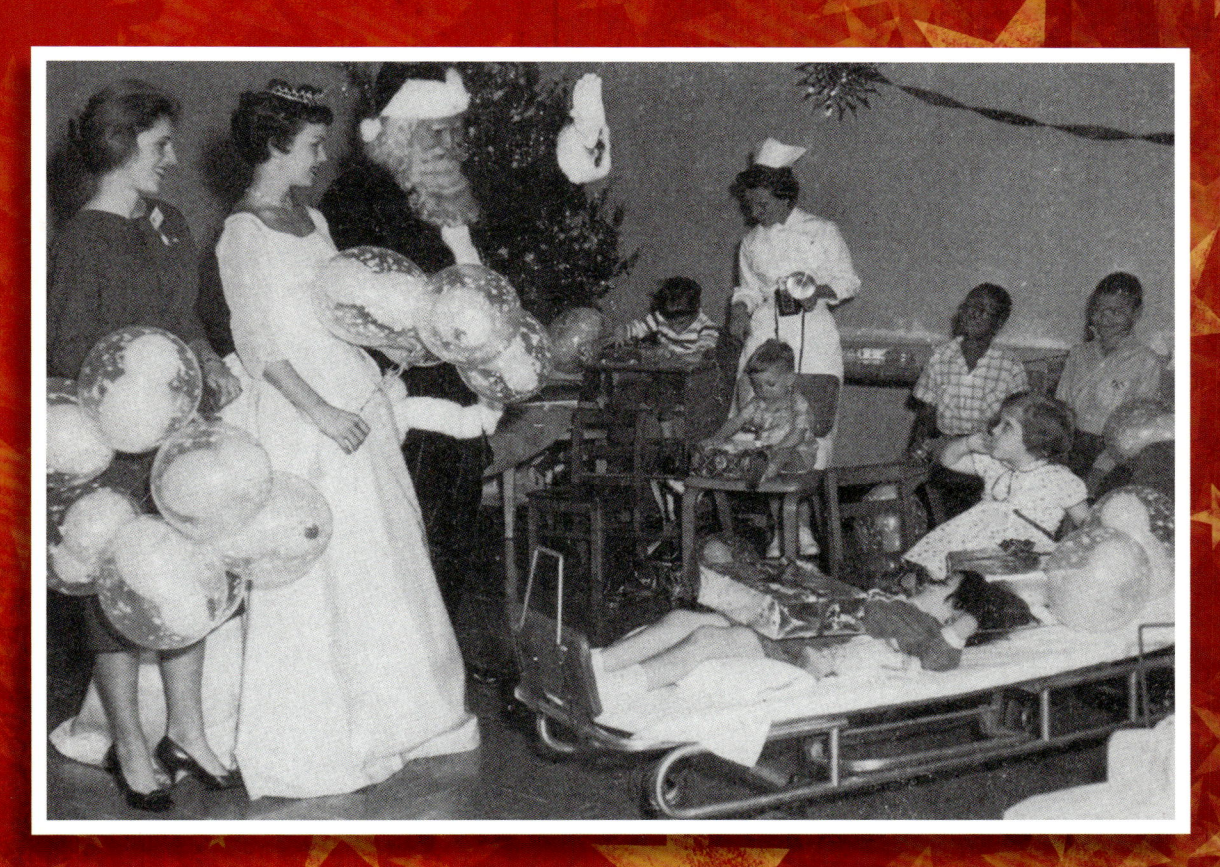

The Snow Queen has often accompanied Santa on his hospital visits. Photo courtesy of Richmond Times-Dispatch.

LEGENDARY SANTA'S STORIES FROM THE CHAIR

Some of the children were terminally ill. Though pale and weak, their faces would light up as we entered their rooms, Snow Queen in her shimmering white gown and me in my red suit with sleigh bells jingling. Seeing the joy of these children immediately swept away any tiredness we had felt from our busy day at Santa Land. It invigorated and inspired us. The hospital may have been a place for broken little bodies, but the Christmas spirit was alive and well among its young patients, their families and the caring staff.

Some might think these visits would be depressing. But I don't feel that way. Rather, they lift me up. One little boy told me, "I hope you have a Merry Christmas, Santa!" I told him "I am having a Merry Christmas because I got to see you!"

Wherever I go, I like to leave the children with the thought that I've made them as happy as they made me!

Legendary Santa goes out into the community on many other occasions and one of my favorites is the Christmas parade. It's had different names and different sponsors, but one thing never changes… Richmonders love their parades! They line the streets, bundled up against the December cold. Setting up folding chairs or laying down blankets, they stake out their spots on the sidewalks. Dads hoist their kids up on their shoulders for a better view of the floats and marching bands. Other spectators perch on rooftops or hang out of windows. Of course my reindeer and sleigh are the last float in the parade so that's the grand finale. Santa and Snow Queen love hearing everyone calling out Merry Christmas!

Santa and the Snow Queen Mary Catherine Piland waving from their sleigh in the Christmas parade.

LEGENDARY SANTA'S STORIES FROM THE CHAIR

Santa has met many Virginia Governors at the Capital Tree Lighting. Clockwise from top left: Gov. Charles Robb, Gov. John Dalton, Gov. Bill Tuck.

The Christmas Tree Lighting at the Capitol building with the Virginia governors has always been a special treat for me. What an honor to meet the governors and their families and to take part in such an impressive ceremony.

The lighting of the tree at the beautiful Jefferson Hotel is always a spectacular occasion. I love walking down those famous steps (supposedly used in Gone with the Wind) with my beautiful Snow Queen.

In 2010, we started a new tradition at a new location. I had the honor of lighting the Christmas tree at West Broad Village in Short Pump. That's the site of the west end location of the Children's Museum of Richmond. What a warm welcome we received there!

96

Santa rides in a horse-drawn carriage after the Capital Tree Lighting ceremony. Photo courtesy of the Richmond Times-Dispatch.

LEGENDARY SANTA'S STORIES FROM THE CHAIR

Mrs. Barbara "Bobbie" Ukrop, with three of her grandchildren, visited Santa in Santa Land. Photo courtesy of the Richmond Times-Dispatch.

Santa and the Snow Queen descend the steps at the Jefferson Hotel at its Christmas Tree Lighting.

LEGENDARY SANTA'S STORIES FROM THE CHAIR

As I look back at my journey over the past seventy-five years, I have to say that some of my happiest memories are about the Santa Train. Sponsored by Miller & Rhoads, it ran from 1958 to 1971 from Richmond to Doswell and back on the tracks then owned by the Richmond, Fredericksburg & Potomac (RF&P) Railroad.

A Miller & Rhoads driver would pick me up early at the store and take me to Ashland. Meanwhile, children and parents, dressed in their holiday outfits, would board the train at the old Broad Street Station, which is now the Science Museum of Virginia. There were twenty-two cars, with some like the old-fashioned Pullmans, provided by the Railroad Historical Society.

The conductor gets ready to let the children board the Santa Train. Photo courtesy of the Ellett family.

Legendary Santa greets a happy young passenger on the Santa Train. Courtesy of Richmond Times-Dispatch.

LEGENDARY SANTA'S STORIES FROM THE CHAIR

I would be waiting on the lawn of Randolph-Macon College with the Snow Queen and my old-fashioned red sleigh when the train arrived in Ashland. I'd see all the children with their noses pressed against the windows looking for me. The Snow Queen and I would hop on the last car and start greeting the kids. Our elves were already on the train, as was Felix the Clown and his little pig. Members of the Miller & Rhoads Teen Board participated as well. A man named Charlie Wakefield played Christmas carols on the accordion. He was blind, but a friend led him up and down the aisles on the train as he entertained his youthful audience.

The train would then travel up to the Doswell Depot where the engine would disconnect, then hook back up and take the train back to Richmond. Snow Queen and I would work our way through those twenty-two cars and speak to every child.

The Santa Train would pull back into Broad Street Station. The luggage vehicle man would give me a ride to the mezzanine level where I would stand on one of those big benches and wish all the boys and girls Merry Christmas as they left. Then the Miller & Rhoads driver would take me back to Ashland to do it all over again. The Santa Train made four round trips that day, so that was eighty-eight

LEGENDARY SANTA'S STORIES FROM THE CHAIR

cars of very excited kids. The train only ran one day out of the season and all four trips were always sold out. I remember that in 1958 you could buy a ticket for seventy-five cents. For many who rode on the Santa Train, that investment provided a priceless memory.

One year it snowed. When the train pulled in to Ashland, the kids saw Santa in his red suit standing on the snowy lawn of Randolph-Macon, waving to them as snowflakes swirled around him. That really made it feel like Christmas!

The Santa Train was discontinued many years ago when Amtrak took over. Yet I feel that it still exists in spirit, running along the indelible tracks of nostalgic memories, transporting its joyful passengers back to a time of childhood wonderment. That grand old train was full of Christmas magic, and next to my sleigh, it carried me on some of the best rides of my life!

Illustration by Herb Wimble

LEGENDARY SANTA'S STORIES FROM THE CHAIR

A Boy and his Grandfather Ride the Santa Train

Like most young boys, Ed Crews loved trains. But he was luckier than most because his grandfather, Dr. Guy R. Harrison, felt the same way. His grandfather often talked about working as a railroad telegraph operator before he went to dental school. Dr. Harrison frequently took his grandson to watch the trains arrive and depart at Broad Street Station.

When his grandfather offered to take him on the Miller & Rhoads Santa Train, Ed knew he was going for the ride of a lifetime. In fact, it was the first trip he'd ever taken that wasn't in a car.

"I remember walking into Broad Street Station with my grandfather," Ed reminisced. "It was cavernous, an immense space that dwarfed a five-year-old boy. In the lobby, there were these oblong benches made of walnut or oak where people sat waiting for their train. The wood was worn smooth, and as a kid, you'd just want to slide down the length of it. In the center of each bench was a wooden platform of sorts which held a model train in a glass case. Those model trains were a source of endless fascination.

"But the best part was when the real Santa Train rumbled into the station. My grandfather took my hand and led me down the ramp to the platform with all the other boys and girls. And there it was! Enveloped in steam and fog, brakes hissing, its enormous bulk clanked and groaned to a stop on the tracks. My grandfather was tall enough to see in the windows, but I was eye-level with that massive undercarriage. I felt very small standing beside the Santa Train with all the noise and hustle and bustle of people coming and going. But my grandfather winked at me and squeezed my hand to reassure me this was all a grand adventure.

"Finally the conductor called 'All aboard!' We found our seats and settled in for the ride to Ashland. I remember framed pictures of Richmond scenes hanging on the walls. At the time, I didn't think about what a uniquely Richmond experience this was, or that, like childhood, it would not last forever.

"As the Santa Train clattered over the tracks, I kept an eagle eye on the door of our car, looking for Santa. Well before St. Nick appeared, some men came through the car. One played an accordion and another sang 'White Christmas.' At last, Santa and the beautiful Snow Queen came walking down the aisle. They stopped at each seat and talked to every single child in the car. Santa really was red-cheeked and jolly. And, the Snow Queen was a spectacular vision in her white sparkly gown. I recall clearly asking Santa for a Fanner 50, a Mattel cap gun that was the most popular toy that year.

"Of course, the best memory was seeing the real Santa on the Santa Train with my grandfather…a Christmas gift that has stayed with me all my life."

Santa and the Snow Queen at Broad Street Station greeting passengers for the Santa Train, 1959. Photo courtesy of the Richmond Times-Dispatch.

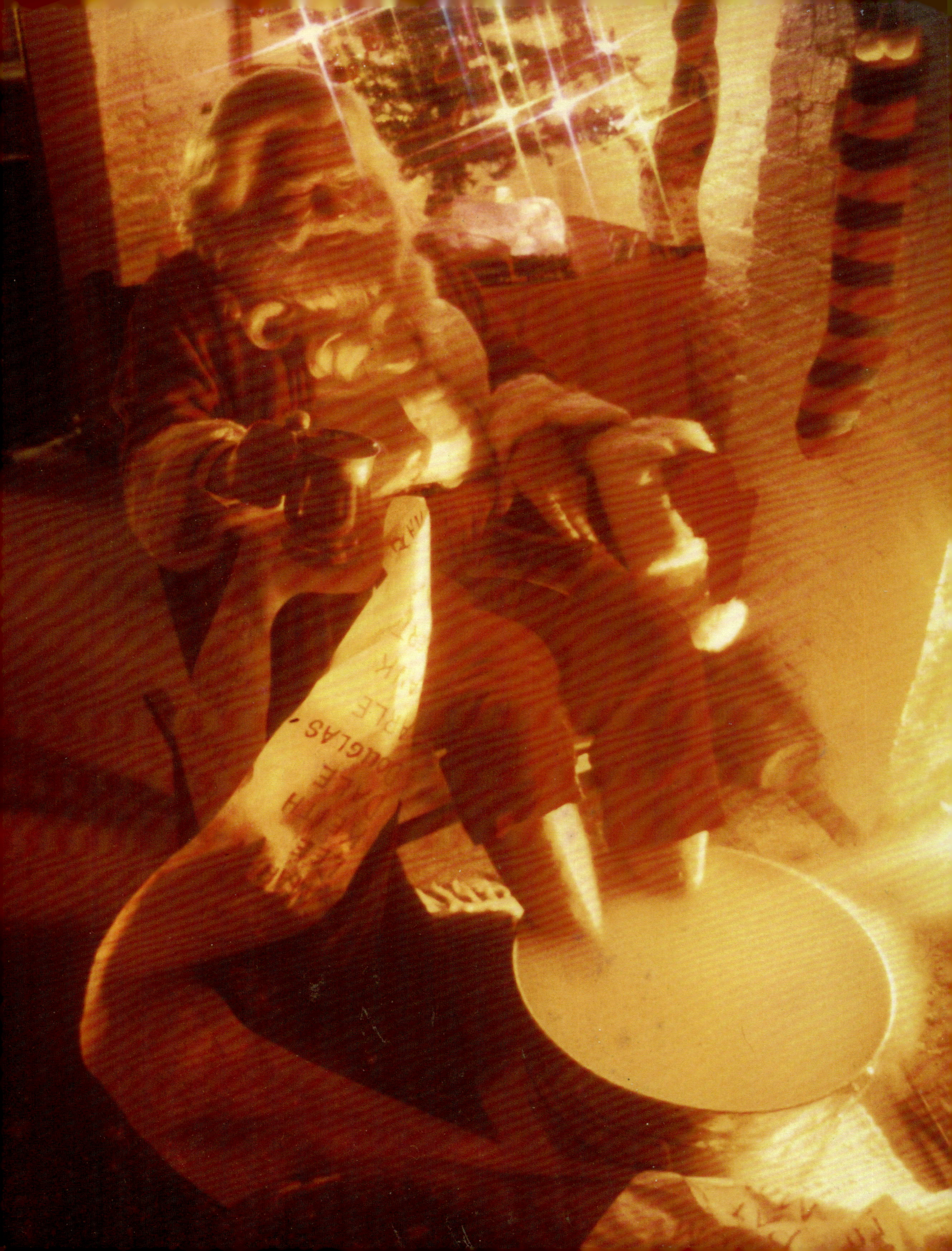
DOUGLAS

Santa's Wish List

Over these many years, children of all ages have given me their Christmas lists. They have shared their wishes for material things and their hopes and dreams for things that cannot be put in a stocking or under a tree. As I tell every one of them, "I will try my best" to bring them what they wish for.

But every once in awhile, someone will ask me "What do you wish for, Santa?"

I'm happy to have the opportunity to tell you.

First and foremost, I wish for all children to have a safe and happy home. I want all children to grow up in families where they are loved, respected and encouraged to always do their best. I wish for their parents to have, as I do, endless patience.

Likewise, I want children to do their part and listen and learn from Mom and Dad. I tell them when they sit in my lap to "Try to be as good as you can." I want to see good behavior, but I don't expect perfect behavior.

I wish for children to experience the joy of Christmas, which is truly the joy of giving. I want them to see that Christmas is more than toys. It's about kindness, goodwill, sharing. It's about giving freely from the heart, without any expectation of getting something back. It's about families having time-honored traditions that knit them together and give them a touchstone they can return to, year after year, generation after generation.

Finally, for as much as children see Legendary Santa as the great giver of gifts, I am the one who receives much more. Not just the homemade ornaments and Christmas cards or cookies that are pressed into my hands as I sit in the chair. I am the recipient of children's awe and wonder, the innocence of their open hearts and open arms. Though I never expect anything back for all the presents I deliver, the love I have received in return far outweighs any material benefit. It makes my job the best in the world!

Santa is ready for a long winter's nap after delivering all the Christmas presents.

LEGENDARY SANTA'S STORIES FROM THE CHAIR

Santa's Secret

Now let me tell you a little secret, one I've kept for seventy-five years. There's something else in my great sack of Christmas presents besides toys and candy canes.

Old Santa takes all the love and devotion expressed by my adopted city of Richmond and uses it to jumpstart my sleigh back to the North Pole and the long trip around the world. That's why I linger those extra moments saying goodbye to all my babies before I go up the chimney on my last day at the Children's Museum.

The belief of Richmonders in the magic of Santa Claus is so powerful that I knew it would carry me and all my reindeer far beyond the city limits! That is one of the many reasons I chose Richmond as my adopted city. And why I have been so happy here for all these years! Richmond's love for Legendary Santa sends me on my way, multiplying itself as my reindeer and I travel the globe so that we can spread love and joy throughout the world!

Thank you, Richmond! And never forget… old Santa loves you!

Santa says the love he receives at his home away from home in Richmond fuels his sleigh for its long journey on Christmas Eve. Photo courtesy of Robin Hood.

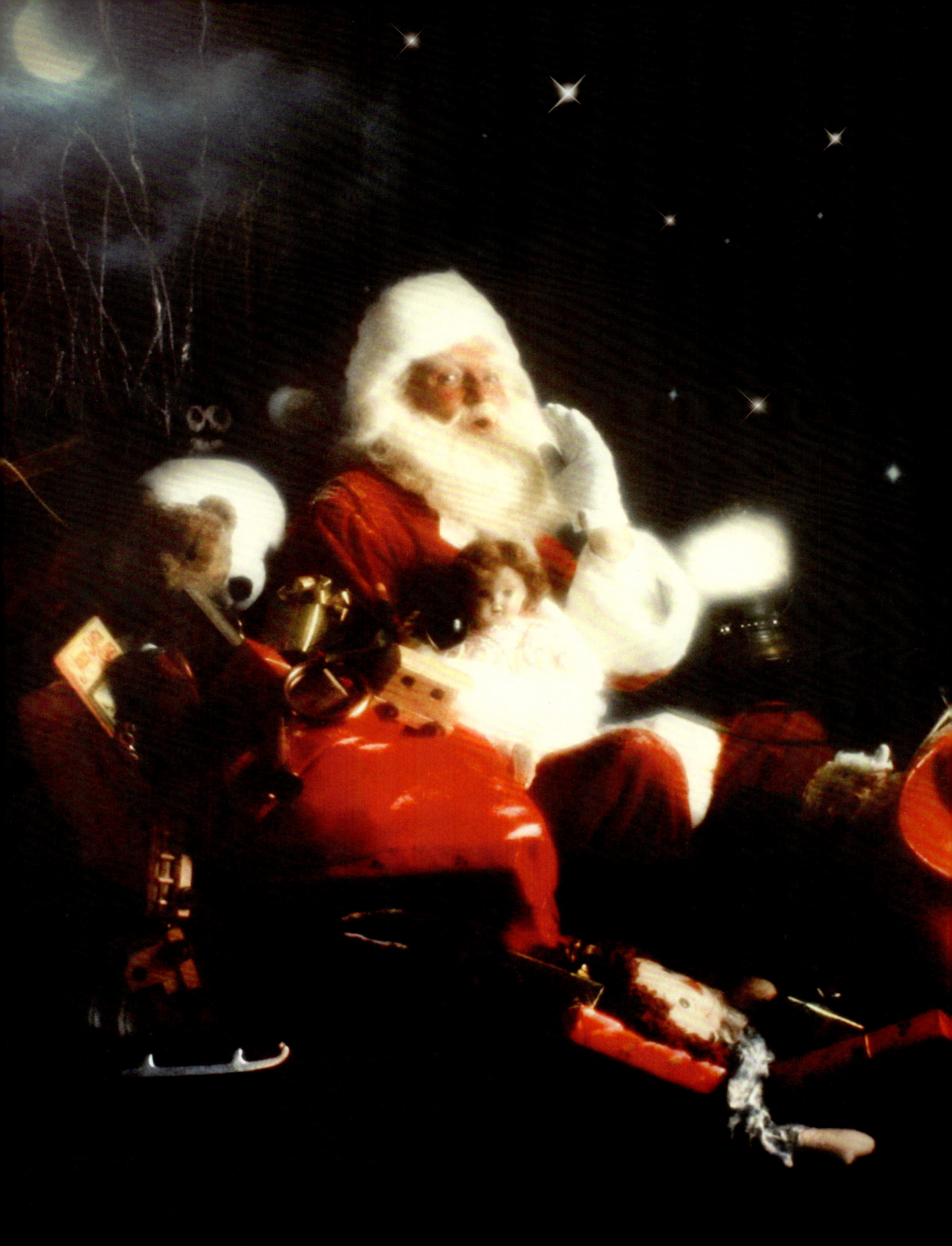

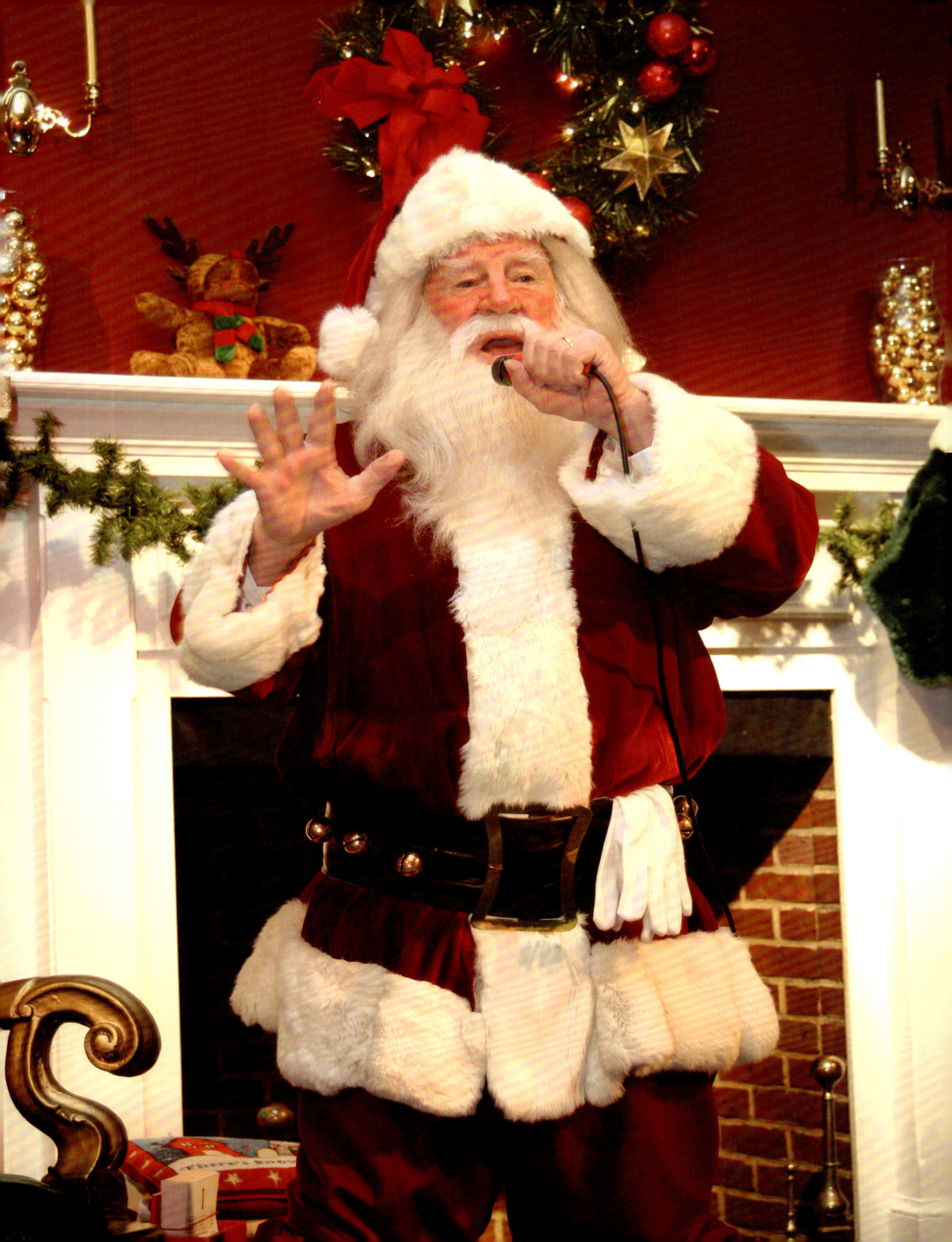

Yes, Virginia, There is a Santa Claus

S Location: The Children's Museum of Richmond, December 24, 2010. It's almost three o'clock on the afternoon of Christmas Eve.

Santa Land is filled with children and parents, just as it has been every day since the day after Thanksgiving. But today, the holiday outfits seems a little dressier and an extra buzz of excitement fills the room.

It's Christmas Eve, the last day of Santa's stay in Richmond. It's the only day he goes back up the chimney to return to the North Pole and make his rounds delivering Christmas presents.

It seems that more families than usual are getting group photos taken with Santa. One family squeezes fourteen people, representing four generations, around Santa's chair. Old Santa, laughing good-naturedly, is barely visible in a sea of red and green dresses and skirts and jackets and vests.

Youngsters eagerly wait for Santa to come down the chimney on Christmas Eve at the Children's Museum of Richmond.

Finally, all the lists have been read and all the pictures have been snapped. Santa gets up from his chair to address his audience. This is his final goodbye for the season. The room grows very quiet.

"Well, boys and girls, it's three o'clock. In a few minutes, I'll be on my way. And tonight, this very night, I'll be coming by your house! So go to sleep early like your Mom tells you," Santa advises.

He pauses a moment. "Now I want to tell you a little story." The emotion is welling in his voice and his rosy cheeks seem to grow a little redder. He takes a few seconds to compose himself. Taking a deep breath, he turns to the Elf and says, "I hope I can get through this."

Santa turns back to the eager faces of the boys and girls watching him on the Santa Land stage. He begins, "This little story was published in the New York Sun in 1897. That was 114 years ago! Here is what it said:

"DEAR EDITOR: I am 8 years old.

"Some of my little friends say there is no Santa Claus.

"Papa says, 'If you see it in THE SUN it's so.'

"Please tell me the truth; is there a Santa Claus?

"VIRGINIA O'HANLON.

"115 WEST NINETY-FIFTH STREET."

VIRGINIA, your little friends are wrong. They have been affected by the skepticism of a skeptical age. They do not believe except [what] they see. They think that nothing can be which is not comprehensible by their little minds. All minds, Virginia, whether they be men's or children's, are little. In this great universe of ours man is a mere insect, an ant, in his intellect, as compared with the boundless world about him, as measured by the intelligence capable of grasping the whole of truth and knowledge.

Yes, VIRGINIA, there is a Santa Claus. He exists as certainly as love and generosity and devotion exist, and you know that they abound and give to your life its highest beauty and joy. Alas! how dreary would be the world if there were no Santa Claus. It would be as dreary as if there were no VIRGINIAS. There would be no childlike faith then, no poetry, no romance to make tolerable this existence. We should have no enjoyment, except in sense and sight. The eternal light with which childhood fills the world would be extinguished.

Not believe in Santa Claus! You might as well not believe in fairies! You might get your papa to hire men to watch in all the chimneys on Christmas Eve to catch Santa Claus, but even if they did not see Santa Claus coming down, what would that prove? Nobody sees Santa Claus, but that is no sign that there is no Santa Claus. The most real things in the world are those that neither children nor men can see. Did you ever see fairies dancing on the lawn? Of course not, but that's no proof that they are not there. Nobody can conceive or imagine all the wonders there are unseen and unseeable in the world.

You may tear apart the baby's rattle and see what makes the noise inside, but there is a veil covering the unseen world which not the strongest man, nor even the united strength of all the strongest men that ever lived, could tear apart. Only faith, fancy, poetry, love, romance, can push aside that *curtain and view and picture the supernal beauty and glory beyond. Is it all real? Ah, VIRGINIA, in all this world there is nothing else real and abiding.*

No Santa Claus! Thank God! he lives, and he lives forever. A thousand years from now, Virginia, nay, ten times ten thousand years from now, he will continue to make glad the heart of childhood.

Legendary Santa recited the famous editorial by heart, word for word. Little did he know that earlier that December, he was visited by someone for whom the "Yes, Virginia" editorial held a very special meaning, one that was even more poignant that particular Christmas.

Carolyn Morgan (now Perrin) served on the Teen Board of Miller & Rhoads and became Miss Teenage Richmond of 1971. She had loved Legendary Santa since she was a child.

"After we saw Legendary Santa, then we could feel like now it's Christmas!" she said of her family's annual visits downtown.

Her love of Santa was so ingrained that it influenced her talent choice when she competed in the Miss Teenage America pageant in Fort Worth, Texas.

"I recited 'Yes, Virginia, There Is a Santa Claus' for my talent," she said.

Carolyn continued the Legendary Santa tradition when she married Rick Perrin and they had their girls – Amanda, Lindsey and Tiffany. "We would stand in line for hours at Miller & Rhoads," she said. Evidently, there was no special treatment in Santa Land for a former Teen Board member!

Carolyn Morgan (Perrin) 1957

LEGENDARY SANTA'S STORIES FROM THE CHAIR

One year the unthinkable happened. "Santa got Lindsey's name wrong!" Carolyn laughed. "He called her Redford! We don't know how that happened!" The incident became a family joke with Redford as a new nickname for Lindsey. At the time, Lindsey worried that she wouldn't get the present she asked for – a "Fluppy" stuffed dog, similar to the popular Pound Puppy – because Santa had confused her name. However Santa redeemed himself and brought her the Fluppy.

Clockwise from left: Amanda, Tiffany and Lindsey Perrin 1985

When Amanda and Lindsey got married and started their own families, their husbands, who were not from Richmond, quickly came to understand that Legendary Santa would be a part of their lives. Amanda and Todd Williams took their girls, Kaitlyn and Sydney, in matching smocked dresses, to see Santa. Lindsey and Jeff Crider would join them with their son Jaxson.

"Tradition was extremely important to Lindsey," Carolyn noted. "When she and Jeff had Jaxson, they took him as an infant to see Legendary Santa in 2008." In 2009, they took him, dressed in an outfit whose colors matched his cousins' dresses.

That was the last time that Lindsey Perrin Crider would see Legendary Santa.

She passed away in April 2010 after a chronic illness that suddenly took a turn for the worse. She was only twenty-nine. Little Jax was only two. The family's grief seemed too much to bear.

When the Christmas season drew near, the Perrins' cherished tradition of going to see Legendary Santa suddenly seemed unimaginable.

"It would have been so much easier just not to go," Carolyn said. "Everything was so hard. Every new experience without Lindsey was so painful."

Nevertheless, in December, the Perrin family went to the Children's Museum of Richmond to honor Lindsey's memory and love of tradition by going to see Legendary Santa. They took little Jaxson and his cousins Kaitlyn and Sydney, once again dressed in coordinated outfits.

Jaxson Perrin and his cousins Kaitlyn and Sydney with Santa 2010.

"Seeing Jax in Santa's lap was like seeing Lindsey in his lap," Carolyn said. "I'm glad we went. It was very healing. I felt like Lindsey knew we were here and that was very comforting."

She recalled what she had told her girls when they started to express doubts about the real existence of Santa. "I told them they can think what they like, but that I have always believed in the magic of Santa Claus." She paused, then added, "That belief is even stronger now."

Thus, holding fast to their beloved tradition in the hardest of times, the Perrin family, having seen Legendary Santa, could feel that now it was Christmas.

His audience clapped appreciatively after Legendary Santa concluded his flawless recital of the "Yes, Virginia" piece by memory. It was finally time to bid farewell to his "babies." Parents and children were reluctant to let him go, even though they knew he had a big job ahead of him that night. Voices shouted out: "Have a safe trip Santa! Santa, we love you!"

"Be as good as you can!" Santa exclaimed, waving with arms outstretched, embracing the outpouring of heartfelt affection and devotion and, with his kindly, benevolent smile, returning it in full measure.

"Merry Christmas! Bye bye, sweethearts!" he called one last time.

Then he turned, strode across the stage and ducked into the chimney. In a moment, his boots left the floor as the audience drew in its collective breath. The boots dangled in the chimney for a second, then in a flash were gone. Sleigh bells jingled in the distance as the Snow Queen said, "And I heard him exclaim as he drove out of sight…."

"Merry Christmas to all and to all a good night!" came Santa's voice as his sleigh climbed into the wintry skies above Richmond.

Thus he left his "home away from home" to make his appointed rounds, having bestowed immeasurable gifts of love, generosity and joy to all those who believe in wonders unseen and unseeable. And, once again, Legendary Santa made glad the heart of childhood … in Richmond, Virginia and throughout the world.

That's enough excitement for one year. Time for a well-deserved rest. Photo courtesy of the Valentine Richmond History Center.